NEW INSIGHTS IN MASS MEDIA

NEW INSIGHTS IN MASS MEDIA

K.B. Datta

AKANSHA PUBLISHING HOUSE
NEW DELHI • GUWAHATI • VISAKHAPATNAM

AKANSHA PUBLISHING HOUSE
4649-B/21, Ansari Road
Darya Ganj, New Delhi - 110 002
Ph.: 23263193 / 9811582579 / 09435116718
Fax: 011-23263193
Email: ektabooks@yahoo.com
www.akanshapublishinghouse.com

New Insights in Mass Media

First Published 2010
ISBN 978-81-8370-235-5

PRINTED IN INDIA

Published by Akansha Publishing House, New Delhi and Printed
Harmain Offset Press

Contents

Preface

> "No man will ever be a big executive who feels that he must, either openly or under cover, follow up every order, he gives and see that is done—nor will he ever develop a capable assistant."
>
> —*John Lee Mahin*

Mass media is the main vehicle of mass communication. In common parlance, Mass media denotes a section of the media specifically designed to reach a very large audience such as the population of a nation-state or entire world. The term was first coined in the 1920s with the advent of nationwide radio networks, mass-circulation newspapers and magazines. However, some forms of mass media such as books and manuscripts had already been in use for centuries.

Tracing the history of mass media, types of drama in numerous cultures were probably the first mass-media, going back into the Ancient World. Movable clay type was invented in 1041 in China. However, due to the slow spread of literacy to the masses in China, and the relatively high cost of paper there, the earliest printed mass-medium was probably European popular prints from about 1400. Although these were produced in huge numbers, very few early examples survive, and even most known to be printed before about 1600 have not survived. Johannes Gutenberg printed the first book on a printing press with movable type in 1453.

This invention transformed the way the world received printed materials, although books remained too expensive really to be called a mass-medium for at least a century after that. Newspapers developed around from 1612, with the first example in English in 1620; but they took until the nineteenth century to reach a mass-audience directly.

Remarkably, during the 20th century, the growth of mass media was driven by technology that allowed the massive duplication of material. Physical duplication technologies such as printing, record pressing and film duplication allowed the duplication of books, newspapers and movies at low prices to huge audiences. Radio and television allowed the electronic duplication of information for the first time. Mass media had the economics of linear replication: a single work could make money. Vast fortunes were to be made in mass media.

As of now, Mass media includes Internet media (like blogs, message boards, podcasts, and video sharing) because individuals now have a means to exposure that is comparable in scale to that previously restricted to a select group of mass media producers. The communications audience has been viewed by some commentators as forming a mass society with special characteristics, notably atomization or lack of social connections, which render it especially susceptible to the influence of modern mass-media techniques such as advertising and propaganda.

Obviously, media nad communication are widely debated topics and a plethora of literature is available on diverse themes. As is suggested by the name of the title we have chosen here some select themes which put now insights into mass media. The main themes included here in are—Mass Media and Public Relations; Insights into Electronic Media; Mass Media and Advertising; Mass Media & Media

Bias; World Wide Web (WWW) and Web Browsing; TELNET: A Modern Way of Communication; Usenet; Internet and Information Technology; Glossary; and Bibliography etc. Hopefully, the contents will enlighten all students, trainers and professionals in the field of mass media and communication.

In fact, this book is devised as a dependable reference handbook for media persons. So the text is supported by well-researched readings, penned by leading experts in the field. Real credit for this ought go to them all. I am deeply beholden to all original contributors, their publishers and sources for subscribing their views. My friends and colleagues have helped me a lot while working on this. I am grateful to them all. Finally, I am thankful to my publisher for bringing out this in elegant manner within shortest possible time.

—Author

1

Mass Media and Public Relations

> " Credit it like a looking glass, which once sullied by a breath, may be wiped clear again; but if once cracked can never be repaired."
>
> —*Scott*

As is gernarally admitted, the news media constitute a major factor in public relations, controlling the flow of publicity through the most important channels of public communication. Good working relations with the editors, reporters, cameraman, broadcasters etc., are essential in securing good publicity coverage. With the increasing number of media and its specilisation, competition for space and time has intensified and publicity has attained a more significant role in public relations. As public relations practitioners have become more professional in their approach to publicity, they develop a community of interest with news writers. Editors are recognising that public relations departments are a source of genuine news and technical information. On the other hand, public relations professionals are acquiring a better knowledge of mass media and operating problems.

Selection of Media

For successful public relations, proper selection of the mass media is must in preparing and placing news releases.

The common practice of indiscriminate mailing of releases and articles is wasteful. Considering the high cost and the excessive waste in worthless releases, the preparation and distribution of publicity must be given greater attention by publicity departments. Systematic collection of information about the audiences and editorial requirements of newspapers, magazines and radio and television stations is essential in reducing the waste.

Newspapers and magazines should be read and broadcasts audited to determine the publicity they use. Editors may be asked for sample copies of their publications for review. Editors may be interviewed at their offices, invited to lunch and tactfully tackled about their editorial policy. Records should be maintained of all periodicals sent for an analysis about the effectiveness of the publicity.

The following media are gernerally used for public relations:

1. Newspapers: Newspapers are the major medium of publicity. They are read by millions, enjoy reader confidence, influence public opinion, appear regularly and intensively cover local and regional areas. Newspapers appeal to the special interests of business executives, women, sports enthusiasts and others through special sections providing opportunities for product publicity on these subjects.

2. Magazines: Magazines are an important medium for product news, feature stories and pictorial publicity. They tend to be read leisurely and thoroughly. In some cases, magazines may be preserved for future reference. The attractive appearance, quality paper and fine colour reproduction of magazines make them ideal for picture publicity.

3. Redio and Television: Radio and TV publicity has

developed rapidly. In this age of science, there can only be a few areas which do not come under the network system of TV/Radio. It is a powerful media and a believable news source having deep impact.

The main tool of public relations is communication. This sounds simple enough but the kind of communication carried on is not the spontaneous communication that takes place when people just sit down and talk to each other. It is purposeful communication that is intended for to change people's attitudes, to motivate them to certain kinds of action. In the hands of those who know how to use this tool effectively it can become a very powerful instrument indeed, and sometimes public relations men have been under fire because some unscrupulous people amongst them have used this instrument to achieve ends that were not socially desirable. But public relations in the true sense of the term involves an identification of the particular interest with the social or public interest.

In fact, communication though it may seem to be a simple phenomena, as a tool of public relations we conceive of communications as a purposeful and organised system intended to achieve certain objectives. It is only when we are able to understand all that the process of communication involves that we will be able to make use of this tool for our own purpose.

The process of communication involves the conception and the sending of the message. It requires an instrument for the conveying of the message which may be the human voice or some other written, printed, visual or audio visual media. It presupposes also the existence of a receiver of the message. The process can only be said to be complete when the receiver of the message has comprehended the meaning of the message sent.

It is, therefore, necessary that the language and the medium of the message should be capable of being understood by the person who receives the message. Unless, therefore, this whole process of conceiving, sending, receiving and comprehending a message is completed, effective communication cannot be said to have taken place. The communications may be of two kinds External and Internal.

External communications are with the financiers, government and parliament, press, dealers and community. Internal communications are within the organisations. The difference between a well managed industry and a badly managed turn out to be a reflection of the sort of communications system operating in them. But it is given a low priority.

It is generally supposed that the kind of communication that has evolved spontaneously in the organisation is the best that could be thought of or in any case adequate for the purpose. Every organisation needs, therefore, to examine carefully whether the system of communication that prevails within is the best suited for its requirements.

Communication Media

It is pertinent to note that media of communication can be divided under three heads. Audio or oral representing those media of communication which are by word of mouth and the visual which includes written, pictorial and symbolic media as well as combinations of both.

House Journal: The house journal is the most popular and, if properly planned, edited and distributed, the most effective medium of communication. The house journal may also be designed for external projection of an organisation or to communicate with dealers, suppliers or other publics. It has got to have the professional approach in its format, periodicity, gathering news, editing, photographs, layout, contents and its distribution.

Advertising

Advertising is a major publuc relations tool used to communicate with both internal and external publics. It has its primary objective of projecting the company as an institution interested in society's welfare as well as to create a favourable public image. PR advertising is used to promote public welfare. For an advertisement to be aimed at public good, it has to fulfil the following steps.

1. It must 'sell' the company as a good place to work with.
2. It must build favourable opinion about the company by stressing the competence of the company's management, the company's accumulated knowledge, manufacturing skills, technological progress and product improvements and its contribution to social advancement.
3. It must educate, inform or impress the public regarding the company's policies, style of functioning facilities, objectives, ideals and standards.

In fact, public relations advertising is an effective medium of communication for several reasons. It is economical since it can transmit PR messages to a varied audiences at a relatively low cost. It can be highly selective and concentrated on a particular segment of public. Quick communication is possible through daily newspapers. Intenvisve local coverage may be secured through newspapers, radio, broadcast and TV.

Practices

Misunderstandings may seriously affect the sales and

profit of the company or the financial support or voluntary aid and so on. Advertisements are used to comet misconceptions by publishing facts about their policies and practices to the public.

Securing and Keeping Good Suppliers

An increasing number of manufacturers and merchants advertise in selling their product to the manufacturers and merchants to invite suppliers to 'open houses' and to promote the welfare of resources.

Creating a Favourable Image of an Organisation

Public relation advertising is used to enhance public confidence in it and its product and services. A company that can create a favourable public attitude can aspire to sell more of its products and services thereby building a loyal dealer organisation.

To Arouse Interest of Stockholders and Financial Community

Corporations advertise in the financial sections of newspapers and in financial magazines to inform shareholders and the financial community about their financial condition.

To Win the Goodwill of Community Neighbours

Institutional advertising is a part of corporate public relations programme. They tell the community about the operations of the firm and its contribution to the welfare of the community. This also highlights the company's role in creating jobs and employment.

To Inform Government Officials

Advertisement is discussing issues involved in pending legislation and to seek the support of the government.

There can also be an appraisal of the issues affecting the company and their community at large.

To Win Goodwill of the Employees

Local newspapers, broadcast and employee magazines are utilised to inform workers about the company, policies, plans accomplishments and future programmes. They are helpful to dispel rumours and create a better climate of understanding.

To Develop Goodwill of Dealers

Trade magazines and mail advertising is used by manufacturers to present their policies, promotions and developments. Advertising in trade publications is also used to guide merchants in better and effective merchandising and sales promotion.

To Inform and Serve Consumers

Consumer magazines, radio and TV reach consumers with information about the company's contribution to public welfare. They also aid consumers in solving problems of contemporary life such as pollution, traffic safety, inflation and equal employment opportunity.

To Improve Labour Relations

Public relations advertising in local newspapers is used to keep employees and community informed about benefits, working conditions and labour policy. It is also used to present management's position in a labour dispute and to dispel misunderstanding of its motives.

To Render Public Service

Advertising is highly used by corporations to promote highway safety, national health and charitable work.

As one of the example the excellent advertising campaign consistently being launched by the Loss Prevention Association can be cited; then there are the General Insurance Corporation, the Life Insurance Corporation of India, the leading Pharmaceutical Manufacturers to educate the public as to how some few diseases can be prevented; baby food manufacturers in their advertising give valuable tips concerning baby care and maternal health.

Research and Evaluation

It must be remembered that the importance of fact-finding is the ultimate aim of any public relations programme or strategy. While knowledge of the basic principles of public relations is an essential precondition for the development of public relations programmes, it is necessary to appreciate that there is no readymade formula that will apply to all situations. In developing and executing a public relations programme for any organisation we have to try to study the specific situation in the context of which the programme has to be developed.

When applying public relations to any organisation, there is need to work out a strategy for the long term as well as for the short term achievement of results. Hence public relations is waging a war to change people's attitudes, overcome prejudices, suspicions and dislikes and establish instead goodwill and understanding. To be successful, a public relations programme will have to proceed through four stages: Fact finding; Planning; Implementation; and Evaluation. It is only through a careful study of all the facts of the situation that public relations objective can be defined. Sources from which facts may be gleaned are press reports and comments, proceedings of the Indian Parliament of State Legislatures, reports of customer reactions obtained from the company's own sale force or from dealers and distributors, employees comments, the kind of response the company gets when it puts out an advertisement for recruitment.

In most cases these will add up to give a fairly clear picture of the kind of image the organisation has, of its weaknesses and strengths. In planning, or working out the strategy various steps that are needed to be taken should be carefully studied. The means of communication to be adopted, an estimation of costs, requirements of manpower etc. are some factors to be given proper thought of.

In all cases, even where the PR man has been authorises to prepare and execute his plans within the frame work of an overall budget, it is desirable to keep top management informed to try to secure their cooperation in the implementation of the plan. In the implementation of the public relations programmes, the definite target audience and media or other media required to influence the people should be examined.

With the precise definition of the audience, the message is likely to get diffused and considerable waste involved. An evaluation has to be made to discover how far the objectives have been achieved. Here again it may be necessary where there is some doubt or controversy with regard to the results to take recourse to the process of formal research.

Having found out the results and the extent to which the objectives originally set have been achieved, the public relations man will move to the next campaign. As such there is, a main theme of public relations programme, being the investigation of facts of the situation, a study of what the problem is and what is involved in an effort to tackle the problem. Systematic fact finding will eliminate all prevailing uncertainties. It is necessary to assemble a basic fact file or each case and to operate continuous intelligency activities constantly adding to the basic fact file. However, there are limitations of research. The findings of research are only meant to provide data to help in decision making. It is not something to be used everywhere in all kinds of situations. Knowing when to use research and how to make use of research is something that requires skill and experience. It has to be remembered that the findings of research are only part of the total informations mix that is required for the planning of public relations strategy.

Research can help point to the management to get an insight into the reasons when certain attitudes develop or change or do not develop. It is also helpful in deciding what is the best media to reach the target desired in the most economic way that too emphatically.

Assessing Effectiveness

Results relative to disciplines like Marketing. Marketing Research, Sales Management and Advertising Operations are tangible as they can be analysed and recorded in arithmetical terms. Such is not the case with Public Relations as the result produced by it is intangible. It is almost like the result produced by Fine Arts like Music, Dance or Drama which can be evaluated by our Ears and Eyes. Public Relations like Fine Arts does not lend itself to evaluation in terms of tangibility and effectiveness.

Code of Corporate Ethics

I. "Our first responsibility is to our customers:

1. Our products and services will always be good, will strive to make them better at lower costs.
2. Customers' orders' will be promptly and

accurately filled.

3. Our dealers will be helped to make a fair profit.

4. Our "after-sales" service will be dependable, and our relations with customers will be cordial.

II. "Our second responsibility will be to those who work with us the men and women in our factories and offices:

1. They will have a sense of security in their jobs.

2. Our wages will be fair and adequate commensurate with the social and economic environment in which we operate.

3. Working hours will be conducive to production and working conditions clean and orderly.

4. There will be opportunity for advacement for those well qualified and experienced.

5. Each employee will be considered, first, as an individual, standing on his or her own dignity and merit.

III. "Our third responsibility is to our Board of Directors.

1. Our executives will be persons of talent, education, experience and ability. They will be persons of common sense and full understanding.

2. Promotions and incentives to employees will be on the basis of 'how good are they to the Corporation; not how good are they to individual bosses.

IV. "Our fourth responsibility is to the 'communities' in which we live.

1. We will help maintain the character of good corporate citizen by supporting good works and charity, and bear our share of taxes.
2. We will endeavour to generate the feeling that all the properties we are privileged to use are ours, first.
3. We will participate in civic improvement (promotion) programmes: health, education and good government, and acquaint the community with our activities.

Further, it must be remembered that there is a big difference between managing and doing. How successful are you in your managerial practice lies in how well could you understand 'managing and 'doing' and go abcut your duties accordingly; and that is the core of Public Relations in Manager Statesmanship.' The manager often finds himself in the position of the interplanetary traveller who doesn't know how fast he is going unite he knows where he is and can't know where he is until he knows how fast he is keeping pace with his activities.

Often the result is that the manager knows that he may have to take refuge in spending most of his time dealing with that which makes his most secure, and administrative problem-solving. In other words, he relies more on doing than managing Not that 'doing' ins't important.

In fact, a manager's doing activities may become more important than his managing activities especially if he has only a couple of subordinates. But there has to be a point where managing activity gets the attention it needs. Only then can a group of individuals be directed and motivated to make a planned contribution toward achievement of group objectives. It's not unusual for the employee to see him 'boss' as a 'father figure'. This is normal. But it can produce difficulties if the boss is not aware of it and doesn't know how to handle it. Meeting of the minds followed by unity in common action is the salient feature of 'public relations in manager statesmanship.

The following contain some tips which may prove of use in this respect:

1. When an authority commands, the group obeys; the result is acquiescence.
2. The manager tells; the staff follows; the result is assent.

Remarkably, in both these situations, the person of higher status secures the compliance of those of lower status. How much the result is based on status and how much on reason or emotional adherence is not always determinable. The manager who has had some insight into public relations knows about the efficiency of using 'orders' depending upon situations.

The following must be practiced;

1. When to' 'Command"
   (a) In case of danger
   (b) For the lazy and indifferent worker
   (c) To the careless man
   (d) When the workman refuses to obey safely orders and rules
   (e) To the agitator
   (f) To the workman who refuses to do the work as he is told
   (g) To stop waste or delay
   (h) To the disobedient worker.

2. When to "Request"
   - (a) To the touchy or sensitive worker
   - (b) To the untrained worker
   - (c) To the nervous, irritable worker
   - (d) To get a little more done
   - (e) To the man who is interested in his work
   - (f) To a person of equal footing
   - (g) first time you reprimand or caution a worker
   - (h) To avoid making a man sore
   - (i) To an older man-in age and service
   - (j) To the "hard-boiled" man
   - (k) To do a difficult job in a particular way.
3. When to "Suggest"—for fully experienced workers
   - (a) When improved methods are sought
   - (b) To the man who is trying to get ahead
   - (c) To the man who is trying to assume responsibility
   - (d) Try it out with a new group of experienced workmen
   - (e) Use it to develop initiative.

Remember it, should be kept in mind that the greater the distance between the give and the receiver of an order, the more likelihood of misunderstanding and the greater the chance of the reaction of the receiver.

Authority, like money, may be saved or squandered. It may be invested for security or for growth. It may be hoarded for its own sake. It may be used up in expendable luxuries. It may produce anything or nothing. If an investor of money is satisfied with security and slow growth, he deposits his savings in a guaranteed bank account and lets other people worry about using it profitably. If he wants his savings to grow faster, he must learn to do more than check the figures in a Pass Book. He must study the whole field of investing, and learn the nature of money as well as what it can do. He must make his own judgements, and abide by them. He must keep accounts; he must know how much he has to invest and where the opportunities for investment are. He must keep close control.

Not all his investments are likely to be successful; he must liquidate his poor investments, salvaging what he can, and re- invest the proceeds to recoup his losses. He must keep something in reserve, in order to lake advantage of unexpected opportunities, but he must realise that idle reserves produce no gains. As a manager, whatever your level, you can handle your authority in much the same way. You can play it safe, or you can invest for growth.

But before you begin to invest authority for rapid returns you must;

(a) take full account of your authority
(b) study the benefits and the risks involved in delegation
(c) learn all you can about the ability and the character of each of your subordinates
(d) use delegation to motivate your subordinates
(e) devise sound methods of reporting and control.
(f) practice delegation at every opportunity

It is a relatively simple matter to "measure" the authority .you hold by virtue of your appointment to the position you now hold. Whether or not the company has given a written description of your position or provided you with a chart of its relationships with other positions in the company, you can quickly determine the areas in which you have complete freedom to decide the course of action.

Before embarking on public relations career, which involves direct or indirect selling your way through life, it is important for the person to get some notion of what empathy is and grasp the significance of the role it plays in one's life.

What is empathy? Webster says it is Imaginative projection of one's own consciousness in another being. In advertising, then it is the Agency representative's it is seeing matters as others see them. It is the executive causing himself to feel as others feel, and even his feelings for them. The empathic executive treats each client in a considerate manner.

His capacity for empathy permits the executive to be sympathetic to the client's attitudes and beliefs, sensitive to the client's hopes and fears, receptive to the client's ideas and reactions, and appreciative of the client's objectives and values. When empathy is operating, the public relations executive thinks in terms of his 'publics', not just himself. He gives his client no impression of conceit, superiority, condecension, criticism, irritation or impatience.

Instead his sincere question is "How can I help the client get what he wants most?" Being an empathic executive is an art—it is an ability a public relations executive must acquire and master if he is to realise his full potential. This takes time, planned practice, experimentation and experience. A public relations executive should want to perfect his skill in this area until his attempts to understand each of his publics' automatic.

Empathy contribute to a public relations executive's success in several ways. It helps making client's relationship better. It fosters greater understanding. Empathy tells an executive when he should be firm and when he should be more restrained when he should talk and when he should remain silent, even whether he should joke or be serious. The empathic public relations executive is more accurate than the non-empathic competitor in interpreting what a client/buyer says or does. Empathy encourages the client to be frank and sincere with the public relations executive, or reveal, instead of conceal. It encourages the client to welcome and even to look forward to subsequent visits with the PR executive because the client considers him an ally and a friend.

Ethics

1. A system of moral principles = the ethics of a culture.
2. The rules of conduct recognised in respect to a particular class of human actions, or a particular group, culture, etc. = medical ethics - Christian ethics.
3. That branch of philosophy dealing with values relating to human conduct with respect to the rightness and wrongness of certain actions and to the goodness and badness of the motives and ends of such actions.

A personal or specific basis of conductor management to adhere to one's principles.

Standards of business conduct, as all ethical standards have their geneses largely in the moral codes of the religious doctrines which are accepted by the particular society. This tends to act as a unifying force toward acceptance of given moral concepts by a majority of the citizens of the society.

Nonetheless, since the answer to any question of morality hinges in the relative and qualitative criteria of "right" and "wrong" the problem of what constitutes proper business and professional conduct is controversial. Just before the dawn of the present century, a discernible change began to occur in the social and economic forces which so strongly influence public opinion of "right" and "wrong". Standards of morality were viewed with a new objectivity, possibly due to the complexity of the developing professions arising from industrial, social and political as well as constraints and the attendant distance between professionals and their clients.

Or perhaps the tremendous increase in the numbers of people practising various professions. Whatever the responsible forces, the fact is that the void between man's three sets of moral standards -his treatment of other people, the treatment he expects others to accord him, and the manner that he thinks others people should treat each other - began to close, and more objective view of standards is in ample evidence. This transition did not result from an overnight conversion of the population to "higher thought", but as with all changes involving people, was a gradual shift to meet the irresistible demands of both economic and social changes. What then is meant by the term "ethical standards of conduct in profession"? Various authorities seem to be in fair agreement as to the general meaning of the term "ethics". That they are not as yet in strict accord is evidenced by the following observations;

In fact, in every field except ethics all kinds of professionals are concerned primarily with things as they are. In ethics, however, they are concerned with things as they ought to be for themselves and their clients. Ethics, or moral responsibility, as it is sometimes called, consists of a body of social laws and theories that has grown and evolved through the ages from as far back in history as man has recorded life.

Ethics, the study of moral principles and conduct: Truth is absolute, but ethical standards are relative; they exist to meet the practical needs of people in varying situations and circumstances. Ethics is the science of conduct. But by no means all of conduct concerns us in a study of Ethics. Clearly a large part of our conduct is without ethical significance-neither good nor bad, right nor wrong, moral nor immoral, except as special conditions may affect the action or its results.

Ethics deals with personal conduct and moral duty and concerns human relations with respect to right and wrong." From these statements we may evolve a definition of ethics that would include the concept that ethics is a code, or set of rules, that determines the degree of lightness of conduct involving oneself, oneself and another person or another group of person.

The use of the ethics code as a measuring device is inherent within the definition and meaning of ethics. The pragmatic application is at once obvious. If the results of a person's conduct are beneficial, good, or at least innocuous, then the conduct is right or ethical. However, the intent a motivating the person conducting himself in a given manner should also be measured. If one intended the results of his conduct to be beneficial or good, then the conduct is right or ethical. However, as quite frequently happens, good results are the fruit of evil intentions and complete fiascos result from the best of inventions; therefore, neither measurement can be used to the exclusion of the other.

In the dynamic world of today's management, where

time for meditating upon the intents of one's conduct is crowded out by the necessity of deciding what future conduct is to be undertaken, only the results of a persons's actions are usually measured in determining if conduct is ethical. In a world of increasing globalization, the media has many potentials. It has the possibility of spreading information to places where in the past it has been difficult to get diverse views. It has the potential to contribute to democratic processes and influences especially on countries and regimes that are not democratic.

On the negative side though, it also has the ability to push the ideas and cultures of more dominant interest. The phenomenon of "cultural imperialism" raises concerns in many countries where people fear that their culture gets diluted or given a back seat to the demands of large media and corporate interests in the name of globalization, where products and imagery, mainly from the west, make it into the televisions and homes of people. The fear of many people is that if people around the world are molded into model consumers, following a western standard, then it is easier for large companies to sell their products and know their buyer's habits etc, while eroding local cultures and traditions.

There is often extensive debate as to how likely this will be, whether local cultures and traditions will exert their influence on local forms of globalization, or if there will be more extremist backlash. In different parts of the world, many of these and other reactions are already seen. A documentary by the Open University in UK, aired on the BBC2 channel, October 29, 2003. The documentary, titled *Images over India* looked at the positive and negative consequences that globalization of media had in India on various parts of society.

Amongst many things, the documentary noted the following:

(a) India is one of the world's largest markets for satellite tv, with some 300 million viewers.

(b) The Indian economy opened up in the 1990s after decades of being closed, (Pressure came from western and international institutions such as the IMF, World Bank, etc.) o This led to an explosion in global consumer goods o There was also an explosion in Indian television

It is noteworthy that with the continuing globalization of television since the 1980s (like CNN, MTV, Sky, Star TV, Sony etc), in India, demand from urban middle classes came around 1991 for the likes of CNN for coverage of international events such as the first Gulf War. With the expansion of cable TV and DTH and other devices, now TV has made access to every nook and corner of the country. Thus this mode of media may prove an efficient vehicle public relations.

2

Insights into Electronic Media

> "Freedom of Press is based on a principle which the whole world must practice if we are to have peace, and that is the principle of tolerance—of being able to stand criticism and of realizing that nobody has the infallible truth."
>
> —*H.C. Lodge*

As we know our present age is the era of knowledge and information and communication technology which have eliminated the yore considerations of gap in time and distance. In fact our's is the age of electronics.

In present chapter we have made an attempt to highlight electronic media and its impact on traditional media. All salient features are described in coherent manner. This will help us understand the real impact of electronics on our media culture as well the historical development of electronic media.

Benjamin Franklin once said, "if all printers were determined not to print anything till the were sure that it would offend nobody, there would be very little printed."

Basically, to communicate with one another is a compulsive urge of human beings. Civilisations and cultures progress to the extent communications have made them possible. Speech has a limited distance range. Communication within the family and very closely living families helped the primitive communities. As movement also was limited, there could have been thousands of languages as despaired in the expression 'babel of tongues.' After speech, the next important development was writing. It helped preservation of ideas, of thoughts, of agreements and their transmission from generation to generation.

Until paper and printing were invented, even writing could help only to a limited extent for communication between far flung communities and societies. Printing helped the multiplication of information and knowledge and their easy availability to tens of thousands of people. Even though paper and printing extended the range of communication, they could not influence the rapidly of transmission. It was only from the middle of the last century that rapid transmission of communications by electrical means became possible. Telegraph helped the transmission of written messages, almost instantaneously, and telephony from 1876 onwards facilitated the transmission of speech, enabling the dissemination of information and knowledge very rapidly.

Telegraphy and telephony are, however, means of communication from one individual to another, from any to any and could be said to be private means of communication. What is transmitted by telegraph or telephone could be known to millions only when it was printed and distributed through newspapers or otherwise. The next quantum jump occurred with the invention of the radio and its utilisation for broadcasting of information from a central source to any and everywhere equipped with a radio receiving device. This is communication from one to many.

Remarkably, by the beginning of the 1930s, almost all over the world radio broadcasting for information transmission over wide communities and areas had been established. From then onwards we could say that the information was becoming more and more electronic-based. In the 1950s began the transmission of picture along with voice for broadcasting. Television increasingly caught on. The black and white pictures were themselves a wonder, but television became an arresting marvel with colour transmissions. It has become increasingly affordable by more and more people because the transistors and the integrated circuits made the mass-produced radios as well as the television sets cheaper every decade. The invention and increased availability of portable recording and replaying devices enabled the capture of events as they were taking place and their near instantaneous broadcasting throughout the world. Communication satellites with the capability of telephony and telex and television helped the worldwide instantaneous transmission of news and views of events.

Before the invention of the telegraph, it took weeks and months for news in one country to be known in other countries and continents. But with the radio and the television, both carried over satellites, distance and time have been so shrunk that information from one continent to another can be transmitted and known in as little time as it takes within a village. In other words, our globe itself has been reduced to a village. Audio and video cassette recording and their multiplication in million is enabling the spread of instruction and training and entertainment and education. One illustration of how an electronics involving education spreading system has come up could be useful. India is having the largest unlettered population, at over 500 million. The school going population is also of the order of hundreds of millions. It all of them are, in the traditional fashion to be sent to schools, the amount of expenditure over buildings, textbooks and transportational programmes can be recorded on video cassettes and broadcast over countrywide or regionwide media through the satellite, we can have very economically, and rapidly propagated education.

What is called 'Projection Television' is a versatile aid. Pictures are reproduced on a very large screen attached to the television monitor, enabling scores of viewers to be instructed with the least expense. Also, instead of libraries of books if there is a library of video cassettes containing text and illustrated and explained by the best teachers, and if these cassettes can be circulated among the schools, the quality of instruction in the village-level schools, which are poorly staffed can be fantastically improved. Electronics, computers and telecommunication media are enabling the simultaneous printing of newspapers from several centres. Electronic book publishing is another rapidly growing activity. Personal computers, access data bases over telecom media and print out a mass of information in whatever format it is wanted. They are a great aid for information storage, retrieval and processing.

In modern times, because of the industrial revolution and intensive and economic exploitation of resources and increasing consumption of goods and services, huge companies or corporations and organisations are a necessity. They are also economically efficient. It is very necessary that all these companies and organisations explain to the masses of money-providers and consumers why and how they are performing and how best their services could be utilised by the consumer.

This is one of the most important aspects of public information and relations that every corporate organisation has to undertake. While newspapers could be useful only a fraction of the 30 per cent of the lettered people in India, mass communication media like radio and television are the most effective and economic means of mass information. Huge organisations become more and more impersonal and bureaucratised. Customers, and may be even the workers, will find themselves helpless in understanding or reacting with these organisations.

Various communication media like audio and video cassettes and electronic reproduction methods enable a public instructional and information programme to be carried out easily. They are the means by which mind can be informed and influenced for the achievement of an organisation's goals and for the transformation of society.

It is apt to mention here that it was the invention of the "movable type" cast in a mould, using an alloy of lead-tin-antimony, by Gutenburg, a German, in 1554, that created a revolution in the medium of mass communication and introduced the term 'printed word' which has become the most potent weapon in the fight against illiteracy and superstition and in spreading knowledge to every nook and corner of the entire world. The traditional method of printing termed the letterpress, started by Gutenburg, using the metal type through the printed message, remained almost unaltered for over 500 years. Any changes that were introduced in the methods or techniques of composing were only in the mechanisation and automation of the typesetting process but not in the basic process of printing by the letterpress method.

With the spread of books, journals and newspapers in the Western countries, after industrial revolution, which required faster typesetting and printing, mechanisation of the typesetting process became an absolute necessity. From hand composing, an entirely manual process of setting individual types, the transition was to mechanical composition, that is, setting types with the help of machines. Several inventors came into this field of typesetting machines between 1820 and 1889 but many of them could not stand the test of time. Only two machines—Linotype (1836) and Monotype (1887) both American, survived the test for fully automatic text setting. With several improvements made constantly, they were serving the printers, particularly the newspaper printer, all over the world, setting types in all the languages in use.

But with the invasion of the electronics on the communication media during the '50s' these hot metal typesetting machines have become completely outmoded and in the advanced countries they have been entirely displaced by computerised phototypesetting machines. This technological revolution in the form of phototypesetting has entered the Indian scene also very recently and will perhaps displace at least 60 per cent of the existing hot metal composing machines before the end of this decade. No one will think of buying hot metal machines any more, as the manufactures have stopped producing them. Let us examine briefly the origin of this electronic revolution in the field of communication and its impact on the printed world. After the World War II, there has been enormous growth in the amount of recorded information, especially in science and technology, which is often referred to as 'information explosion.'

This created a need for information storage and retrieval systems vastly different from the traditional method of the printed book which was too slow to keep pace with the information explosion. One of the effects of this greatly expanded quantity of information is the development of specialisation. There is so much to know about so many things that nobody can encompass everything known about a major field. Therefore, one tries to segment the field, learn it in summary or outline form and concentrate on a subfield in detail, which is specialisation.

As the information of every major field increases enormously and the areas of specialisation widen in greater proportion, the traditional method of storing the information in printed books becomes uneconomical, processing the information time consuming and location and retrieval of the stored information much laborious. Thus arose the obvious need for a new way of processing the information at a fast pace, which will also permit subsequent location and retrieval as quickly as possible. This was how electronics came into the field of information processing. Though originally the systems were developed with scientific and technical communication specifically in mind, these were further developed to accommodate other kinds of scholarly and professional informational information transfer.

It is new technology and a technological revolution, much of it electronic or related to electronics and computers. A whole range of new equipments, methods and techniques have been developed in the past few years for every segment of our system of communication through the printed word. Though initially these changes were more technological than conceptual, the sweeping technological changes have already started encouraging new concepts and new modes of communication.

Some of the new methods and techniques which can be said recent yet revolutionary developments are as follows:

1. Electronic document creation and editing which includes word processing and computerised text editing.
2. Phototypesetting with a wide variety of direct entry, on line and off line computerised systems.

3. New imaging and reprographic techniques such as electronic printing, microform publication and laser electrographic printing.
4. Electronic communication including electronic mail, electronic publication and electronic journals.
5. New recording, storage and retrieval system like holographic storage, bubble memories and so on.

Now question arises—what is the impact of these electronic media on the printed word and what changes have they introduced in the traditional method of producing the printed product? The first of these has been to alter the nature of the basic product. In the traditional technology, the printed word was the one and only product. But with the introduction of the computer and the electronic media, the fundamental product was now a data base. It was no longer the printed word but a precise, manipulable, compact record which could be used with considerably flexibility for various applications, including that of the printed product. The first impact is then the development of an electronic literature, a term used very loosely. The new technology makes possible ways of presenting information that were previously unthinkable—creating enormous user searchable bibliographic and numeric data bases stored in interactive computer systems as well as electronic message systems. Publication such as dictionaries, telephone directories, trade can now be revised, updated, subdivided and raised with a degree of flexibility never before known.

Only the computers which drive the phototypesetters today make all this practical. It is also now possible for the text or data bases created on a word processor or computer in one location to be transmitted electronically to a compatible device in another location simply through the conventional telephone lines or internet. An author, for example, can sit at home, use his word processor to create a machine readable record in the form of a magnetic disc, transfer this text data to the printing press located far away through the telephone lines and the printing, using an interfere, can transfer this data to the phototypesetter which produces the author's copy in the form of a film negative or a photographic paper positive in the shape of final page proofs. By this means, the publishers and the typesetting operator are both eliminated and the author directly produces the printed word and the printer carries out only the platemaking and printing on the press.

Though the entry of electronics has vastly changed the printing machinery, processes and techniques, in a general way, its greatest impact is in the area of typesetting only. In fact, phototypesetters have not only revolutionised the typesetting process but have changed the very structure of the printing industry as such. With the introduction of phototypesetters of the first generation in the beginning of 50s, we have come to the fourth generation of phototypesetters in the beginning of the 80s. These are electronic marvels, very highly sophisticated and capable of things beyond the common man's comprehension. Many factors outside the printing industry have played a dominant role in bringing out these third and fourth generation photosetters. They include: computers, micro-computers, micro-processors, lasers, digitisation of information, screen-based technology including television and telecommunications.

To define in simple language, phototypesetters are machines which produce images on photographic film or paper as negative or positive., in the design required for the printed page. They have suitable devices to store the characters, to select and expose them in the required size, form and measure on the film or paper. The first generation machines (1946-50) were just the replica of the hot metal machines and the operation was mechanical. The second generation machines hold negative film masters of characters on a disc or drum and use optical system, such as zoom lense or turret lens, to vary the type size. They were partly mechanical, partly electronic. The third generation machines are wholly electronic and use cathode ray tube (CRT) for the projection of characters. The characters are digitised and stored in magnetic discs. They can be electronically enlarged, reduced, slanted and emboldened. Digitisation also provides the potential of producing picture as well as text. The fourth generation typesetter use lasers for imaging. Resolution is 1000 dots per inch and output speeds of about *1000 newspaper lines per minute* can be achieved.

Today we have a proliferation of these phototypesetters that are manufactured with a system and modular approach, so that a buyer can instal a simple system according to his present needs and expand it periodically to suit his growing needs. The direct entry photosetter is the simplest of these machines and an Indian firm has started manufacturing this in India in collaboration with the foreign manufacturer. Then we have the online systems, offline systems and page makeup systems.

The common feature of all phototypesetting machines is the input system to capture the author's words in the form of digital data, which can be manipulated and fed into the photosetter to produce the printed word. Key-boards are still the principal means of capturing the text, which are based on the 'Qwerty' standard typewriter layout, with a number of additional function and command keys besides the usual alphabet, punctuation marks and numerals. In the offline and online systems the key-boards, which are attached to a central computer directly or indirectly, are termed the front-end system. Most of these systems were developed initially for use in newspapers, as they have been mainly responsible for taking the initiative in changing over to new technology.

Again the question arises—will the printed word survive the analysis of electronic invasion? There are skeptic who believe that there is no future for the printed word, produced in the traditional way for over 500 years. They predict that there will be a world-wide paper shortage in the next century and printing of books will be extremely costly and electronic publishing of both books and newspapers will be very much cheaper. Though the actual events based on the experience of past may disprove this belief, it is still anyone's guess.

Some damage has already been done displacing the printed word in several areas. Here are some of these: Microform publication of Micropublishing and Microlibraries are the dreams of the future which may completely displace the printed book. The dream is of a library housed in a catalogue cabinet. The "microfiche book" is a development that has come to stay and the computer output microfiche has enlarged its scope. As an indication of the space saving capacity of micropublication, a library in UK contains some 58,000 pages of data on 800 microfiches, each 105 x 148 mm. filled in a cabinet 7 in. by 6 in. by 10 in.

The microfiche service could be more rapidly updated than the printed issues could ever be. Hence, where continuous updating of information is essential, such as in legal, professional practice and financial compilation microform publication has become an established competitively priced medium. Synoptic publishing and simultaneous publishing are two recent developments in periodical and learned journal publishing using microfiche.

With the phenomenal advancement already made in the micro-computers and further dramatic developments expected which will increase their capacity for information storage and retrieval at a much reduced cost, the micro-computer is potentially a teaching device and may become the teaching machine of the future. In educational settings it will be used for information retrieval, information giving, problem solving, manipulation of mathematical models, simulation of different experiments and so on. Using programmed learning techniques and with its capacity for interaction with the learner, the mirocomputer could eliminate the paper based text or the traditional printed book, when all the students are enabled to have easy access to it. For home-based education too, data transmission systems already developed and in use in the Western countries, like PRESTEL of the British Government Post Office, CEEFAX, ORACLE, BBC and ITV data systems would be used. When these are developed further as high-power interactive systems, they will have many more possible implications for educational use. It is likely that correspondence courses of the future run by universities-institutes would switch to such a system at the expense of the printed textbooks.

These systems would seem to virtually climate the need for the printed word since they can supply text, diagram and equations on the video terminal and also offer an inter-active element with information storage and retrieval facilities.

Electronic Newspaper

The electronic newspaper is already a reality in almost all countries, which brings the electronic information to the very doorsteps of the subscriber. *The Columbia Despatch* became the first newspaper in US to go electronic on 1st July 1980 by making almost fall of its editorial product available to the house and business computer subscribers. The subscriber has a television terminal in his house connected to the newspaper office through telephone lines. They call it 'Cable TV.' When the subscriber dials the newspaper office and turns on the Video terminal, the latest edition of the newspaper appears on the screen. Any particular portion of the newspaper like sports, entertainment, market reports, retail shopping, etc. can be called up on the screen by pressing the coded keys. That is the electronic newspaper which has eliminated the printed word. Several other forms of interactive home electronic information system have been introduced in America and Europe by newspapers and press agencies in several cities for transmission of information of all sorts through the Cable TV system. Electronic telephone directory was introduced in France on an experimental basis in 1981 to provide telephone directory information via video terminals in lieu of the printed directories. Subscribers have access to all information in both the yellow and white page directories, more than one quarter million entries including advertising. If this and other experiments prove successful, all of France's 30 million subscribers will get free videotex terminals instead of printed telephone directories, by the early 1990s. One can understand how traditional printers will be greatly affected by the loss of such huge quantity print orders.

A Paperless book has been published by a California publisher. The entire text of the *Computer Cookbook* is available in a disk, and customers can sign on to their own computer terminals for viewing the pages by paying a fee. A US school book publisher estimates that by the end of this decade about one-third of its sales will come from computer-related equipment. Every computer or computerised equipment that is put on the market every day is more powerful than its predecessor and also much smaller in size and cheaper in price. Personal computers, word processors and video terminals may become household items during the 90s. Their capabilities will become hundred-fold. The impact of having a remote terminal in every office and house could be all pervasive. Printers will have to silently witness vast quantities of information bypass the traditional ink-on-paper process to go the route of instantly updatable, random access videopoint.

A wide range of electronic communication technology which can bring about a meaningful revolution and improvement in information transmission are now available. Many of the organisations in developing countries, may not be in a position to make use of all the latest innovations. The developing countries in collaboration with large business organisations should chalk out a phased programme for introduction of new communication devices into their organisational structure to make communication effective. Radio, television, audio-cassettes, video-cassettes, video-tape, videodiscs, telidon, cyclops, video, videotex, etc., are the important innovations. The most significant new technologies are those based on the silicon chip, the laser, fibre optics and the set of technologies known as bio-technologies.

It is necessary to introduce such latest and sophisticated communication technology in collaboration with other countries. The managements in developing countries must realise the importance of new communication technologies for speedy, quick, correct and low cost transmission as well as for imparting education to catch up with the advanced countries of the world.

Both television and radio are electronic media. On the other hand they form second group of advertising commercial media. In this chapter we present in some depth electronic media other than radio and television as well as film existing in communication field. Here we shall investigate the unique nature of electronic media in communication. Geoff Potter points out satellite and its impact on distance education: "In some cases, hermes (The Satellite) brought people together in a way that was a every bit as emotionally moving as it was intellectually stimulating. In other cases students became bored, technical problems made effective interaction impossible, information seemed colourless and static." Griffin points out some basic faults in 'mouth to mouth' communication. They refer to the problems of duration, speed, absence of visual clues, unidimension, absence of phatic communication and disembodiment. According to Griffin, the role of the coordinator is very crucial and very difficult in a satellite programme.

Mass media assistance is required to communicate development programmes and achievements to the mass. Thus today ninety per cent of the population in the country is covered by television.

3

Mass Media and Advertising

> "Intelligent, effective advertising is not an expense it is insusance against the loss of business that the other fellow is fighting for."
>
> *—F.D.Van Amburgh*

While studying mass media, one should understand fully the role of advertisement, a popular vehicle of mass communication. In common parlance, advertising is a form of communication that typically attempts to persuade potential customers to purchase or to consume more of a particular brand of product or service. Modern advertising developed with the rise of mass production in the late 19th and early 20th centuries. Many advertisements are designed to generate increased consumption of those products and services through the creation and reinvention of the "brand image.

For these purposes, advertisements sometimes embed their persuasive message with factual information. Every major medium is used to deliver these messages, including television, radio, cinema, magazines, newspapers, video games, the Internet, carrier bags and billboards. Advertising is often placed by an advertising agency on behalf of a company or other organization. Organizations that frequently spend large sums of money on advertising that sells what is not, strictly speaking, a product or service include political parties, interest groups, religious organizations, and military recruiters. Non-profit organizations are not typical advertising clients, and may rely on free modes of persuasion, such as public service announcements.

Remarkably, the expenses on advertising has increased dramatically in recent years. In 2007, spending on advertising has been estimated at over $150 billion in the United States and $385 billion worldwide, and the latter to exceed $450 billion by 2010. While advertising can be seen as necessary for economic growth, it is not without social costs. Unsolicited Commercial Email and other forms of spam have become so prevalent as to have become a major nuisance to users of these services, as well as being a financial burden on internet service providers.

To begin, it is worth mentioning that Egyptians used papyrus to make sales messages and wall posters. Commercial messages and political campaign displays have been found in the ruins of Pompeii and ancient Arabia. Lost and found advertising on papyrus was common in Ancient Greece and Ancient Rome. Wall or rock painting for commercial advertising is another manifestation of an ancient advertising form, which is present to this day in many parts of Asia, Africa, and South America. The tradition of wall painting can be traced back to Indian rock art paintings that date back to 4000 BCE.

As the towns and cities of the Middle Ages began to grow, and the general populace was unable to read, signs that today would say cobbler, miller, tailor or blacksmith would use an image associated with their trade such as a boot, a suit, a hat, a clock, a diamond, a horse shoe, a candle or even a bag of flour. Fruits and vegetables were sold in the city square from the backs of carts and wagons and their proprietors used street callers or town criers to announce their whereabouts for the convenience of the endusers.

Notably, education became an apparent need and reading, as well printing developed, advertising expanded to include handbills. In the 17th century advertisements started to appear in weekly newspapers in England. These early print advertisements were used mainly to promote books and newspapers, which became increasingly affordable with advances in the printing press; and medicines, which were increasingly sought after as disease ravaged Europe. However, false advertising and so-called "quack" advertisements became a problem, which ushered in the regulation of advertising content. As the economy expanded during the 19th century, advertising grew alongside. In the United States, the success of this advertising format eventually led to the growth of mail-order advertising. In June 1836, French newspaper *La Presse* is the first to include paid advertising in its pages, allowing it to lower its price, extend its readership and increase its profitability and the formula was soon copied by all titles.

Around 1840, Volney Palmer established a predecessor to advertising agencies in Boston. Around the same time, in France, Charles-Louis Havas extended the services of his news agency, Havas to include advertisement brokerage, making it the first French group to organize. At first, agencies were brokers for advertisement space in newspapers. N. W. Ayer & Son was the first full-service agency to assume responsibility for advertising content. N.W. Ayer opened in 1869, and was located in Philadelphia. At the turn of the century, there were few career choices for women in business; however, advertising was one of the few. Since women were responsible for most of the purchasing done in their household, advertisers and agencies recognized the value of women's insight during the creative process. In fact, the first American advertising to use a sexual sell was created by a woman – for a soap product. Although tame by today's standards, the advertisement featured a couple with the message "The skin you love to touch". In the early 1920s, the first radio stations were established by radio equipment manufacturers and retailers who offered programs in order to sell more radios to consumers. As time passed, many non-profit organizations followed suit in setting up their own radio stations, and included: schools, clubs and civic groups.

When the practice of sponsoring programs was popularised, each individual radio program was usually sponsored by a single business in exchange for a brief mention of the business' name at the beginning and end of the sponsored shows. However, radio station owners soon realised they could earn more money by selling sponsorship rights in small time allocations to multiple businesses throughout their radio station's broadcasts, rather than selling the sponsorship rights to single businesses per show. This practice was carried over to television in the late 1940s and early 1950s. A fierce battle was fought between those seeking to commercialise the radio and people who argued that the radio spectrum should be considered a part of the commons – to be used only non-commercially and for the public good.

The United Kingdom pursued a public funding model for the BBC, originally a private company, the British Broadcasting Company, but incorporated as a public body by Royal Charter in 1927. In Canada, advocates like Graham Spry were likewise able to persuade the federal government to adopt a public funding model, creating the Canadian

Broadcasting Corporation. However, in the United States, the capitalist model prevailed with the passage of the Communications Act of 1934 which created the Federal Communications Commission. To placate the socialists, the U.S. Congress did require commercial broadcasters to operate in the "public interest, convenience, and necessity". Public broadcasting now exists in the United States due to the 1967 Public Broadcasting Act which led to the Public Broadcasting Service and National Public Radio. In the early 1950s, the DuMont Television Network began the modern trend of selling advertisement time to multiple sponsors. Previously, DuMont had trouble finding sponsors for many of their programs and compensated by selling smaller blocks of advertising time to several businesses.

This eventually became the standard for the commercial television industry in the United States. However, it was still a common practice to have single sponsor shows, such as The United States Steel Hour. In some instances the sponsors exercised great control over the content of the show - up to and including having one's advertising agency actually writing the show. The 1960s saw advertising transform into a modern approach in which creativity was allowed to shine, producing unexpected messages that made advertisements more tempting to consumers' eyes. The Volkswagen ad campaign—featuring such headlines as "Think Small" and "Lemon" —ushered in the era of modern advertising by promoting a "position" or "unique selling proposition" designed to associate each brand with a specific idea in the reader or viewer's mind. This period of American advertising is called the Creative Revolution and its archetype was William Bernbach who helped create the revolutionary Volkswagen ads among others. Some of the most creative and long-standing American advertising dates to this period.

Remarkably, the late 1980s and early 1990s saw the introduction of cable television and particularly MTV. Pioneering the concept of the music video, MTV ushered in a new type of advertising: the consumer tunes in *for* the advertising message, rather than it being a by-product or afterthought. As cable and satellite television became increasingly prevalent, specialty channels emerged, including channels entirely devoted to advertising, such as QVC, Home Shopping Network, and ShopTV Canada. Marketing through the Internet opened new frontiers for advertisers and contributed to the "dot-com" boom of the 1990s.

Entire corporations operated solely on advertising revenue, offering everything from coupons to free Internet access. At the turn of the 21st century, a number of websites including the search engine Google, started a change in online advertising by emphasizing contextually relevant, unobtrusive ads intended to help, rather than inundate, users.

This has led to a plethora of similar efforts and an increasing trend of interactive advertising. The share of advertising spending relative to GDP has changed little across large changes in media. For example, in the U.S. in 1925, the main advertising media were newspapers, magazines, signs on streetcars, and outdoor posters. Advertising spending as a share of GDP was about 2.9 percent. By 1998, television and radio had become major advertising media. Nonetheless, advertising spending as a share of GDP was slightly lower.

Remarkbly, a recent advertising innovation is "guerrilla marketing", which involve unusual approaches such as staged encounters in public places, giveaways of products such as cars that are covered with brand messages, and interactive advertising where the viewer can respond to become part of the advertising message. This reflects an increasing trend of interactive and "embedded" ads, such as via product placement, having consumers vote through text messages, and various innovations utilizing social network services such as MySpace. Mobile billboards are truck- or blimp-mounted billboards or digital screens. These can be dedicated vehicles built solely for carrying advertisements along routes preselected by clients, or they can be specially-equipped cargo trucks. The billboards are often lighted; some being backlit, and others employing spotlights.

Some billboard displays are static, while others change; for example, continuously or periodically rotating among a set of advertisements.

Pratically, mobile displays are used for various situations in metropolitan areas throughout the world, including: (a) Target advertising; (b) One-day, and long-term campaigns; (c) Conventions; (d) Sporting events; (e) Store openings and similar promotional events; (f) Big advertisements from smaller companies ; and (g) Others. The same advertising techniques used to promote commercial goods and services can be used to inform, educate and motivate the public about non-commercial issues, such as HIV/AIDS, political ideology, energy conservation, religious recruitment, and deforestation. Advertising, in its non-commercial guise, is a powerful educational tool capable of reaching and motivating large audiences. "Advertising justifies its existence when used in the public interest - it is much too powerful a tool to use solely for commercial purposes."

Public service advertising, non-commercial advertising, public interest advertising, cause marketing, and social marketing are different terms for (or aspects of) the use of sophisticated advertising and marketing communications techniques (generally associated with commercial enterprise) on behalf of non-commercial, public interest issues and initiatives. Public service advertising reached its height during World Wars I and II under the direction of several governments

Types of Advertisement

1. Media: Commercial advertising media can include wall paintings, billboards, street furniture components, printed flyers and rack cards, radio, cinema and television adverts, web banners, mobile telephone screens, shopping carts, web popups, skywriting, bus stop benches, human billboards, magazines, newspapers, town criers, sides of buses, banners attached to or sides of airplanes ("logojets"), in-flight advertisements on seatback tray tables or overhead storage bins, taxicab doors, roof mounts and passenger screens, musical stage shows, subway platforms and trains, elastic bands on disposable diapers, stickers on apples in supermarkets, shopping cart handles (grabertising), the opening section of streaming audio and video, posters, and the backs of event tickets and supermarket receipts. Any place an "identified" sponsor pays to deliver their message through a medium is advertising. One way to measure advertising effectiveness is known as Ad Tracking.

This advertising research methodology measures shifts in target market perceptions about the brand and product or service. These shifts in perception are plotted against the consumers' levels of exposure to the company's advertisements and promotions. The purpose of Ad Tracking is generally to provide a measure of the combined effect of the media weight or spending level, the effectiveness of the media buy or targeting, and the quality of the advertising executions or creative.

2. Covert Advertising: Covert advertising is when a product or brand is embedded in entertainment and media. For example, in a film, the main character can use an item or other of a definite brand, as in the movie *Minority Report*, where Tom Cruise's character John Anderton owns a phone with the *Nokia* logo clearly written in the top corner, or his watch engraved with the *Bulgari* logo. Another example of advertising in film is in *I, Robot*, where main character played by Will Smith mentions his *Converse* shoes several times, calling them "classics," because the film is set far in the future. *I, Robot* and *Spaceballs* also showcase futuristic cars with the *Audi* and *Mercedes-Benz* logos clearly displayed on the front of the vehicles.

Cadillac chose to advertise in the movie *The Matrix Reloaded*, whicn as a result contained many scenes in which Cadillac cars were used. Similarly, product placement for Omega Watches, Ford, VAIO, BMW and Aston Martin cars are featured in recent James Bond films, most notably *Casino Royale*.

3. Television Commercials: The TV commercial is generally considered the most effective mass-market advertising format, as is reflected by the high prices TV networks charge for commercial airtime during popular TV events. The annual Super Bowl football game in the United States is known as the most prominent advertising event on television. The average cost of a single thirty-second TV spot during this game has reached $3 million (as of 2009). The majority of television commercials feature a song or jingle that listeners soon relate to the product. Virtual advertisements may be inserted into regular television programming through computer graphics.

It is typically inserted into otherwise blank backdrops or used to replace local billboards that are not relevant to the remote broadcast audience. More controversially, virtual billboards may be inserted into the background where none exist in real-life. Virtual product placement is also possible.

*4. **Infomercials:*** There are two types of infomercials, described as long form and short form. Long form infomercials have a time length of 30 minutes. Short form infomercials are 30 seconds to 2 minutes long. Infomercials are also known as direct response television (DRTV) commercials or direct response marketing. The main objective in an infomercial is to create an impulse purchase, so that the consumer sees the presentation and then immediately buys the product through the advertised toll-free telephone number or website.

Infomercials describe, display, and often demonstrate products and their features, and commonly have testimonials from consumers and industry professionals. Some well known companies in the infomercial business are Script to Screen, Hawthorne Direct International Shopping Network and Guthy-Renker.

*5. **Celebrities:*** This type of advertising focuses upon using celebrity power, fame, money, popularity to gain recognition for their products and promote specific stores or products. Advertisers often advertise their products, for example, when celebrities share their favourite products or wear clothes by specific brands or designers. Celebrities are often involved in advertising campaigns such as television or print adverts to advertise specific or general products.

Approaches

It is remarkable that increasingly, other media are overtaking television because of a shift towards consumer's usage of the Internet as well as devices such as TiVo.

Advertising on the World Wide Web is a recent phenomenon. Prices of Web-based advertising space are dependent on the "relevance" of the surrounding web content and the traffic that the website receives.

E-mail advertising is another recent phenomenon. Unsolicited bulk E-mail advertising is known as "spam". Some companies have proposed placing messages or corporate logos on the side of booster rockets and the International Space Station. Controversy exists on the effectiveness of subliminal advertising, and the pervasiveness of mass messages.

Publicity advertising (also called unpaid advertising), can provide good exposure at minimal cost. Personal recommendations ("bring a friend", "sell it"), spreading buzz, or achieving the feat of equating a brand with a common noun (in the United States, "Xerox" = "photocopier", "Kleenex" = tissue, "Vaseline" = petroleum jelly, "Hoover" = vacuum cleaner, "Nintendo" (often used by those exposed to many video games) = video games, and "Band-Aid" = adhesive bandage) — these can be seen as the pinnacle of any advertising campaign. However, some companies oppose the use of their brand name to label an object. Equating a brand with a common noun also risks turning that brand into a genericized trademark - turning it into a generic term which means that its legal protection as a trademark is lost. As the mobile phone became a new mass media in 1998 when the first paid downloadable content appeared on mobile phones in Finland, it was only a matter of time until mobile advertising followed, also first launched in Finland in 2000.

By 2007 the value of mobile advertising had reached $2.2 billion and providers such as Admob delivered billions of mobile ads. More advanced mobile ads include banner ads, coupons, Multimedia Messaging Service picture and video messages, advergames and various engagement marketing campaigns.

A particular feature driving mobile ads is the 2D Barcode, which replaces the need to do any typing of web addresses, and uses the camera feature of modern phones to gain immediate access to web content. 83 percent of Japanese mobile phone users already are active users of 2D barcodes. A new form of advertising that is growing rapidly is social network advertising. It is online advertising with a focus on social networking sites. This is a relatively immature market, but it has shown a lot of promise as advertisers are able to take advantage of the demographic information the user has provided to the social networking site. Friendertising is a more precise advertising term in which people are able to direct advertisements toward others directly using social network service. From time to time, The CW Television Network airs short programming breaks called "Content Wraps," to advertise one company's product during an entire commercial break.

The CW pioneered "content wraps" and some products featured were Herbal Essences, Crest, Guitar Hero II, CoverGirl, and recently Toyota.

An Analysis

In fact, criticism of advertising is closely linked with criticism of media and often interchangeable. They can refer to its audio-visual aspects (e. g. cluttering of public spaces and airwaves), environmental aspects (e. g. pollution, oversize packaging, increasing consumption), political aspects (e. g. media dependency, free speech, censorship), financial aspects (costs), ethical/moral/social aspects (e. g. sub-conscious influencing, invasion of privacy, increasing consumption and waste, target groups, certain products, honesty) and, of course, a mix thereof. Some aspects can be subdivided further and some can cover more than one category. As advertising has become increasingly prevalent in modern Western societies, it is also increasingly being criticized.

A person can hardly move in the public sphere or use a medium without being subject to advertising. Advertising occupies public space and more and more invades the private sphere of people, many of which consider it a nuisance. "It is becoming harder to escape from advertising and the media. ... Public space is increasingly turning into a gigantic billboard for products of all kind. The aesthetical and political consequences cannot yet be foreseen." Hanno Rauterberg in the German newspaper 'Die Zeit' calls advertising a new kind of dictatorship that cannot be escaped.

"There are ads in schools, airport lounges, doctors offices, movie theaters, hospitals, gas stations, elevators, convenience stores, on the Internet, on fruit, on ATMs, on garbage cans and countless other places. There are ads on beach sand and restroom walls. One of the ironies of advertising in our times is that as commercialism increases, it makes it that much more difficult for any particular advertiser to succeed, hence pushing the advertiser to even greater efforts. Within a decade advertising in radios climbed to nearly 18 or 19 minutes per hour; on prime-time television the standard until 1982 was no more than 9.5 minutes of advertising per hour, today it's between 14 and 17 minutes. With the introduction of the shorter 15-second-spot the total amount of ads increased even more dramatically. Ads are not only placed in breaks but e. g. also into baseball telecasts during the game itself. They flood the internet, a market growing in leaps and bounds.

Other growing markets are "product placements" in entertainment programming and in movies where it has become standard practice and "virtual advertising" where products get placed retroactively into rerun shows. Product billboards are virtually inserted into Major League Baseball broadcasts and in the same manner, virtual street banners or logos are projected on an entry canopy or sidewalks, for example during the arrival of celebrities at the 2001 Grammy Awards.

Critics equate the growing amount of advertising with a "tidal wave" and restrictions with "damming" the flood. Kalle Lasn, one of the most outspoken critics of advertising on the international stage, considers advertising "the most prevalent and toxic of the mental pollutants. From the moment your radio alarm sounds in the morning to the wee hours of late-night TV microjolts of commercial pollution flood into your brain at the rate of around 3,000 marketing messages per day. Every day an estimated twelve billion display ads, 3 million radio commercials and more than 200,000 television commercials are dumped into North America's collective unconscious".

More recent developments are video games incorporating products into their content, special commercial patient channels in hospitals and public figures sporting temporary tattoos. A method unrecognisable as advertising is so-called "guerrilla marketing" which is spreading 'buzz' about a new product in target audiences. Cash-strapped U.S. cities do not shrink back from offering police cars for advertising. A trend, especially in Germany, is companies buying the names of sports stadiums. The Hamburg soccer Volkspark stadium first became the AOL Arena and then the HSH Nordbank Arena. The Stuttgart Neckarstadion became the Mercedes-Benz Arena, the Dortmund Westfalenstadion now is the Signal Iduna Park. The former SkyDome in Toronto was renamed Rogers Centre.

Other recent developments are, for example, that whole subway stations in Berlin are redesigned into product halls and exclusively leased to a company. Düsseldorf even has 'multi-sensorial' adventure transit stops equipped with loudspeakers and systems that spread the smell of a detergent. Swatch used beamers to project messages on the Berlin TV-tower and Victory column, which was fined because it was done without a permit. The illegality was part of the scheme and added promotion. It's standard business management knowledge that advertising is a pillar, if not "the" pillar of the growth-orientated free capitalist economy. "Advertising is part of the bone marrow of corporate capitalism." "Contemporary capitalism could not function and global production networks could not exist as they do without advertising."

For communication scientist and media economist Manfred Knoche at the University of Salzburg, Austria, advertising isn't just simply a 'necessary evil' but a 'necessary elixir of life' for the media business, the economy and capitalism as a whole. Advertising and mass media economic interests create ideology. Knoche describes advertising for products and brands as 'the producer's weapons in the competition for customers' and trade advertising, e. g. by the automotive industry, as a means to collectively represent their interests against other groups, such as the train companies.

In his view editorial articles and programmes in the media, promoting consumption in general, provide a 'cost free' service to producers and sponsoring for a 'much used means of payment' in advertising.

Christopher Lasch argues that advertising leads to an overall increase in consumption in society; "Advertising serves not so much to advertise products as to promote consumption as a way of life."

Obviously, Advertising is equated with constitutionally guaranteed freedom of opinion and speech. Therefore criticizing advertising or any attempt to restrict or ban advertising is almost always considered to be an attack on fundamental rights (First Amendment in the USA) and meets the combined and concentrated resistance of the business and especially the advertising community.

"Currently or in the near future, any number of cases are and will be working their way through the court system that would seek to prohibit any government regulation of ... commercial speech (e. g. advertising or food labelling) on the grounds that such regulation would violate citizens' and corporations' First Amendment rights to free speech or free press."

An example for this debate is advertising for tobacco or alcohol but also advertising by mail or fliers (clogged mail boxes), advertising on the phone, in the internet and advertising for children. Various legal restrictions concerning spamming, advertising on mobile phones, addressing children, tobacco, alcohol have been introduced by the US, the EU and various other countries. Not only the business community resists restrictions of advertising. Advertising as a means of free expression has firmly established itself in western society. Surveys e. g. reveal that advertising is generally seen as a welcome information and seldom as a nuisance.

At worst it is seen as a necessary evil to be endured and most often its entertaining value is pointed out. Hardly any by-law restricting advertising fails to appease possible critics by pointing out the positive effects and the necessity of advertising in its foreword. McChesney argues, that the government deserves constant vigilance when it comes to such regulations, but that it is certainly not "the only antidemocratic force in our society. ...corporations and the wealthy enjoy a power every bit as immense as that enjoyed by the lords and royalty of feudal times" and "markets are not value-free or neutral; they not only tend to work to the advantage of those with the most money, but they also by their very nature emphasize profit over all else....Hence, today the debate is over whether advertising or food labelling, or campaign contributions are speech...if the rights to be protected by the First Amendment can only be effectively employed by a fraction of the citizenry, and their exercise of these rights gives them undue political power and undermines the ability of the balance of the citizenry to exercise the same rights and/or constitutional rights, then it is not necessarily legitimately protected by the First Amendment."

In addition, "those with the capacity to engage in free press are in a position to determine who can speak to the great mass of citizens and who cannot". Critics in turn argue, that advertising invades privacy which is a constitutional right. For, on the one hand, advertising physically invades privacy, on the other, it increasingly uses relevant, information-based communication with private data assembled without the knowledge or consent of consumers or target groups. For Georg Franck at Vienna University of Technology advertising is part of what he calls "mental capitalism", taking up a term (mental) which has been used by groups concerned with the mental environment, such as Adbusters. Franck blends the "Economy of Attention" with Christopher Lasch's culture of narcissm into the mental capitalism: In his essay

Advertising at the Edge of the Apocalypse", Sut Jhally writes: "20th century advertising is the most powerful and sustained system of propaganda in human history and its cumulative cultural effects, unless quickly checked, will be responsible for destroying the world as we know it.

Advertising has developed into a billion-dollar business on which many depend. In 2006 391 billion were spent worldwide for advertising. In Germany, for example, the advertising industry contributes 1.5% of the gross national income; the figures for other developed countries are similar. Thus, advertising and growth are directly and causally linked. As far as a growth based economy can be blamed for the harmful human lifestyle (affluent society) advertising has to be considered in this aspect concerning its negative impact, because its main purpose is to raise consumption. "The industry is accused of being one of the engines powering a convoluted economic mass production system which promotes consumption."

Attention and attentiveness have become a new commodity for which a market developed. "The amount of attention that is absorbed by the media and redistributed in the competition for quotas and reach is not identical with the amount of attention, that is available in society. The total amount circulating in society is made up of the attention exchanged among the people themselves and the attention given to media information. Only the latter is homogenised by quantitative measuring and only the latter takes on the character of an anonymous currency."

According to Franck, any surface of presentation that can guarantee a certain degree of attentiveness works as magnet for attention, e. g. media which are actually meant for information and entertainment, culture and the arts, public space etc. It is this attraction which is sold to the advertising business.

The German Advertising Association stated that in 2007 30.78 billion Euros were spent on advertising in Germany, 26% in newspapers, 21% on television, 15% by mail and 15% in magazines. In 2002 there were 360.000 people employed in the advertising business. The internet revenues for advertising doubled to almost 1 billion Euros from 2006 to 2007, giving it the highest growth rates. Spiegel-Online reported that in the USA in 2008 for the first time more money was spent for advertising on internet (105.3 billion US dollars) than on television (98.5 billion US dollars).

The largest amount in 2008 was still spent in the print media (147 billion US dollars). For that same year, Welt-Online reported that the US pharmaceutical industry spent almost double the amount on advertising (57.7 billion dollars) than it did on research (31.5 billion dollars).

But Marc-André Gagnon und Joel Lexchin of York University, Toronto, estimate that the actual expenses for advertising are higher yet, because not all entries are recorded by the research institutions. Not included are indirect advertising campaigns such as sales, rebates and price reductions. Few consumers are aware of the fact that they are the ones paying for every cent spent for public relations, advertisements, rebates, packaging etc. since they ordinarily get included in the price calculation.

Remarkably, the most important element of advertising is not information but suggestion more or less making use of associations, emotions (appeal to emotion) and drives dormant in the sub-conscience of people, such as sex drive, herd instinct, of desires, such as happiness, health, fitness, appearance, self-esteem, reputation, belonging, social status, identity, adventure, distraction, reward, of fears (appeal to fear), such as illness, weaknesses, loneliness, need, uncertainty, security or of prejudices, learned opinions and comforts. "All human needs, relationships, and fears – the deepest recesses of the human psyche – become mere means for the expansion of the commodity universe under the force of modern marketing. With the rise to prominence of modern marketing, commercialism – the translation of human relations into commodity relations – although a phenomenon intrinsic to capitalism, has expanded exponentially."'Cause-related marketing' in which advertisers link their product to some worthy social cause has boomed over the past decade. Advertising exploits the model role of celebrities or popular figures and makes deliberate use of humour as well as of associations with colour, tunes, certain names and terms. Altogether, these are factors of how one perceives himself and one's self-worth.

In his description of 'mental capitalism' Franck says, "the promise of consumption making someone irresistible is the ideal way of objects and symbols into a person's subjective experience. Evidently, in a society in which revenue of attention moves to the fore, consumption is drawn by one's self-esteem. As a result, consumption becomes 'work' on a person's attraction. From the subjective point of view, this 'work' opens fields of unexpected dimensions for advertising. Advertising takes on the role of a life councillor in matters of attraction.

For advertising critics another serious problem is that "the long standing notion of separation between advertising and editorial/creative sides of media is rapidly crumbling" and advertising is increasingly hard to tell apart from news, information or entertainment. The boundaries between advertising and programming are becoming blurred. According to the media firms all this commercial involvement has no influence over actual media content, but, as McChesney puts it, "this claim fails to pass even the most basic giggle test, it is so preposterous." Advertising draws "heavily on psychological theories about how to create subjects, enabling advertising and marketing to take on a 'more clearly psychological tinge' (Miller and Rose, 1997, cited in Thrift, 1999, p. 67).

Increasingly, the emphasis in advertising has switched from providing 'factual' information to the symbolic connotations of commodities, since the crucial cultural premise of advertising is that the material object being sold is never in itself enough. Even those commodities providing for the most mundane necessities of daily life must be imbued with symbolic qualities and culturally endowed meanings via the 'magic system (Williams, 1980) of advertising. In this way and by altering the context in which advertisements appear, things 'can be made to mean "just about anything"' (McFall, 2002, p. 162) and the 'same' things can be endowed with different intended meanings for different individuals and groups of people, thereby offering mass produced visions of individualism." Before advertising is done, market research institutions need to know and describe the target group in order to exactly plan and implement the advertising campaign and to achieve the best possible results.

A whole array of sciences directly deal with advertising and marketing or is used to improve its effects. Focus groups, psychologists and cultural anthropologists are '"de rigueur"' in marketing research". Vast amounts of data on persons and their shopping habits are collected, accumulated, aggregated and analysed with the aid of credit cards, bonus cards, raffles and, last but not least, internet surveying.

With increasing accuracy this supplies a picture of behaviour, wishes and weaknesses of certain sections of a population with which advertisement can be employed more selectively and effectively.

The efficiency of advertising is improved through advertising research. Universities, of course supported by business and in co-operation with other disciplines, mainly Psychiatry, Anthropology, Neurology and behavioural sciences, are constantly in search for ever more refined, sophisticated, subtle and crafty methods to make advertising more effective. "Neuromarketing is a controversial new field of marketing which uses medical technologies such as functional Magnetic Resonance Imaging — not to heal, but to sell products. Advertising and marketing firms have long used the insights and research methods of psychology in order to sell products, of course. But today these practices are reaching epidemic levels, and with a complicity on the part of the psychological profession that exceeds that of the past. The result is an enormous advertising and marketing onslaught that comprises, arguably, the largest single psychological project ever undertaken.

Yet, this great undertaking remains largely ignored by the American Psychological Association." Almost all mass media are advertising media and many of them are exclusively advertising media and, with the exception of public service broadcasting are privately owned. Their income is predominantly generated through advertising; in the case of newspapers and magazines from 50 to 80%. Public service broadcasting in some countries can also heavily depend on advertising as a source of income (up to 40%).

In the view of critics no media that spreads advertisements can be independent and the higher the proportion of advertising, the higher the dependency. This dependency has "distinct implications for the nature of media content.... In the business press, the media are often referred to in exactly the way they present themselves in their candid moments: as a branch of the advertising industry." In addition, the private media are increasingly subject to mergers and concentration with property situations often becoming entangled and opaque.

This development, which Henry A. Giroux calls an "ongoing threat to democratic culture", by itself should suffice to sound all alarms in a democracy. Five or six advertising agencies dominate this 400 billion U.S. dollar global industry. "Journalists have long faced pressure to shape stories to suit advertisers and owners .... the vast majority of TV station executives found their news departments 'cooperative' in shaping the news to assist in 'non-traditional revenue development." Negative and undesired reporting can be prevented or influenced when advertisers threaten to cancel orders or simply when there is a danger of such a cancellation.

Media dependency and such a threat becomes very real when there is only one dominant or very few large advertisers. The influence of advertisers is not only in regard to news or information on their own products or services but expands to articles or shows not directly linked to them. In order to secure their advertising revenues the media has to create the best possible 'advertising environment'. Another problem considered censorship by critics is the refusal of media to accept advertisements that are not in their interest. A striking example of this is the refusal of TV stations to broadcast ads by Adbusters. Groups try to place advertisements and are refused by networks.

It is principally the viewing rates which decide upon the programme in the private radio and television business.

"Their business is to absorb as much attention as possible. The viewing rate measures the attention the media trades for the information offered. The service of this attraction is sold to the advertising business" and the viewing rates determine the price that can be demanded for advertising.

While critics basically worry about the subtle influence of the economy on the media, there are also examples of blunt exertion of influence. The US company Chrysler, before it merged with Daimler Benz had its agency, PentaCom, send out a letter to numerous magazines, demanding them to send, an overview of all the topics before the next issue is published to "avoid potential conflict". Chrysler most of all wanted to know, if there would be articles with "sexual, political or social" content or which could be seen as "provocative or offensive". PentaCom executive David Martin said: "Our reasoning is, that anyone looking at a 22.000 $ product would want it surrounded by positive things. There is nothing positive about an article on child pornography."

In another example, the USA Network held top-level ‚off-the-record' meetings with advertisers in 2000 to let them tell the network what type of programming content they wanted in order for USA to get their advertising."

Television shows are created to accommodate the needs for advertising, e. g. splitting them up in suitable sections. Their dramaturgy is typically designed to end in suspense or leave an unanswered question in order to keep the viewer attached. The movie system, at one time outside the direct influence of the broader marketing system, is now fully integrated into it through the strategies of licensing, tie-ins and product placements.

The prime function of many Hollywood films today is

to aid in the selling of the immense collection of commodities. The press called the 2002 Bond film 'Die Another Day' featuring 24 major promotional partners an 'ad-venture' and noted that James Bond "now has been 'licensed to sell.

As it has become standard practise to place products in motion pictures, it "has self-evident implications for what types of films will attract product placements and what types of films will therefore be more likely to get made". Advertising and information are increasingly hard to distinguish from each other. "The borders between advertising and media .... become more and more blurred.... What August Fischer, chairman of the board of Axel Springer publishing company considers to be a 'proven partnership between the media and advertising business' critics regard as nothing but the infiltration of journalistic duties and freedoms". According to RTL-executive Helmut Thoma "private stations shall not and cannot serve any mission but only the goal of the company which is the 'acceptance by the advertising business and the viewer'. The setting of priorities in this order actually says everything about the 'design of the programmes' by private television."

Patrick Le Lay, former managing director of TF1, a private French television channel with a market share of 25 to 35%, said: There are many ways to talk about television. But from the business point of view, let's be realistic: basically, the job of TF1 is, e. g. to help Coca Cola sell its product. (...) For an advertising message to be perceived the brain of the viewer must be at our disposal. The job of our programmes is to make it available, that is to say, to distract it, to relax it and get it ready between two messages. It is disposable human brain time that we sell to Coca Cola."

As the result of these dependencies a widespread and

fundamental public debate about advertising and its influence on information and freedom of speech is difficult to obtain, at least through the usual media channels; otherwise these would saw off the branch they are sitting on. "The notion that the commercial basis of media, journalism, and communication could have troubling implications for democracy is excluded from the range of legitimate debate" just as "capitalism is off-limits as a topic of legitimate debate in U.S. political culture". An early critic of the structural basis of U.S. journalism was Upton Sinclair with his novel. The Brass Check in which he stresses the influence of owners, advertisers, public relations, and economic interests on the media. James Rorty wrote: "The gargoyle's mouth is a loudspeaker, powered by the vested interest of a two-billion dollar industry, and back of that the vested interests of business as a whole, of industry, of finance. It is never silent, it drowns out all other voices, and it suffers no rebuke, for it is not the voice of America? That is its claim and to some extent it is a just claim..."

Performances, exhibitions, shows, concerts, conventions and most other events can hardly take place without sponsoring. The increasing lack arts and culture they buy the service of attraction. Artists are graded and paid according to their art's value for commercial purposes. Corporations promote renown artists, therefore getting exclusive rights in global advertising campaigns. Broadway shows, like 'La Bohème' featured commercial props in its set. Advertising itself is extensively considered to be a contribution to culture. Advertising is integrated into fashion. On many pieces of clothing the company logo is the only design or is an important part of it. There is only little room left outside the consumption economy, in which culture and art can develop independently and where alternative values can be expressed. A last important sphere, the universities, is under strong pressure to open up for business and its interests. Competitive sports have become unthinkable without sponsoring and there is a mutual dependency. High income with advertising is only possible with a comparable number of spectators or viewers. On the other hand, the poor performance of a team or a sportsman results in less advertising revenues. Jürgen Hüther and Hans-Jörg Stiehler talk about a 'Sports/ Media Complex which is a complicated mix of media, agencies, managers, sports promoters, advertising etc. with partially common and partially diverging interests but in any case with common commercial interests. The media presumably is at centre stage because it can supply the other parties involved with a rare commodity, namely public attention.

In sports "the media are able to generate enormous sales in both circulation and advertising." "Sports sponsorship is acknowledged by the tobacco industry to be valuable advertising. A Tobacco Industry journal in 1994 described the Formula One car as 'The most powerful advertising space in the world'. .... In a cohort study carried out in 22 secondary schools in England in 1994 and 1995 boys whose favourite television sport was motor racing had a 12.8% risk of becoming regular smokers compared to 7.0% of boys who did not follow motor racing."

Not the sale of tickets but transmission rights, sponsoring and merchandising in the meantime make up the largest part of sports association's and sports club's revenues with the IOC (International Olympic Committee) taking the lead. The influence of the media brought many changes in sports including the admittance of new 'trend sports' into the Olympic Games, the alteration of competition distances, changes of rules, animation of spectators, changes of sports facilities, the cult of sports heroes who quickly establish themselves in the advertising and entertaining business because of their media value and last but not least, the naming and renaming of sport stadiums after big companies. As a major drawback, we Notice every visually perceptible place has potential for advertising. Especially urban areas with their structures but also landscapes in sight of through fares are more and more turning into media for advertisements.

Signs, posters, billboards, flags have become decisive factors in the urban appearance and their numbers are still on the increase. "Outdoor advertising has become unavoidable. Traditional billboards and transit shelters have cleared the way for more pervasive methods such as wrapped vehicles, sides of buildings, electronic signs, kiosks, taxis, posters, sides of buses, and more.

Digital technologies are used on buildings to sport 'urban wall displays'. In urban areas commercial content is placed in our sight and into our consciousness every moment we are in public space. The German Newspaper 'Zeit' called it a new kind of 'dictatorship that one cannot escape'. Over time, this domination of the surroundings has become the "natural" state. Through long-term commercial saturation, it has become implicitly understood by the public that advertising has the right to own, occupy and control every inch of available space.

The steady normalization of invasive advertising dulls the public's perception of their surroundings, re-enforcing a general attitude of powerlessness toward creativity and change, thus a cycle develops enabling advertisers to slowly and consistently increase the saturation of advertising with little or no public outcry." The massive optical orientation toward advertising changes the function of public spaces which are utilised by brands.

Urban landmarks are turned into trademarks. The highest pressure is exerted on renown and highly frequented public spaces which are also important for the identity of a city. Urban spaces are public commodities and in this capacity they are subject to "aesthetical environment protection", mainly through building regulations, heritage protection and landscape protection. "It is in this capacity that these spaces are now being privatised. They are peppered with billboards and signs, they are remodelled into media for advertising."

Basically, Advertising has an "agenda setting function" which is the ability, with huge sums of money, to put consumption as the only item on the agenda. In the battle for a share of the public conscience this amounts to non-treatment (ignorance) of whatever is not commercial and whatever is not advertised for. Advertsing should be reflection of society norms and give clear picture of taget market. Spheres without commerce and advertising serving the muses and relaxation remain without respect. With increasing force advertising makes itself comfortable in the private sphere so that the voice of commerce becomes the dominant way of expression in society."

Advertising critics see advertising as the leading light in our culture. Sut Jhally and James Twitchell go beyond considering advertising as kind of religion and that advertising even replaces religion as a key institution. "Corporate advertising (or is it commercial media?) is the largest single psychological project ever undertaken by the human race. Yet for all of that, its impact on us remains unknown and largely ignored. When I think of the media's influence over years, over decades, I think of those brainwashing experiments conducted by Dr. Ewen Cameron in a Montreal psychiatric hospital in the 1950s. The idea of the CIA-sponsored "depatterning" experiments was to outfit conscious, unconscious or semiconscious subjects with headphones, and flood their brains with thousands of repetitive "driving" messages that would alter their behaviour over time....Advertising aims to do the same thing."

Advertising is especially aimed at young people and children and it increasingly reduces young people to consumers. For Sut Jhally it is not "surprising that something this central and with so much being expended on it should become an important presence in social life. Indeed, commercial interests intent on maximizing the consumption of the immense collection of commodities have colonized more and more of the spaces of our culture.

For instance, almost the entire media system (television and print) has been developed as a delivery system for marketers its prime function is to produce audiences for sale to advertisers. Both the advertisements it carries, as well as the editorial matter that acts as a support for it, celebrate the consumer society. The movie system, at one time outside the direct influence of the broader marketing system, is now fully integrated into it through the strategies of licensing, tie-ins and product placements. The prime function of many Hollywood films today is to aid in the selling of the immense collection of commodities. As public funds are drained from the non-commercial cultural sector, art galleries, museums and symphonies bid for corporate sponsorship.

Similarly effected is the education system and advertising is increasingly penetrating schools and universities. Cities, such as New York, accept sponsors for public playgrounds. "Even the pope has been commercialized ... The pope's 4-day visit to Mexico in ...1999 was sponsored by Frito-Lay and PepsiCo. The industry is accused of being one of the engines powering a convoluted economic mass production system which promotes consumption. As far as social effects are concerned it does not matter whether advertising fuels consumption but which values, patterns of behaviour and assignments of meaning it propagates. Advertising is accused of hijacking the language and means of pop culture, of protest movements and even of subversive criticism and does not shy away from scandalizing and breaking taboos (e. g. Benneton).

This in turn incites counter action, what Kalle Lasn in 2001 called "Jamming the Jam of the Jammers". Anything goes. "It is a central social-scientific question what people can be made to do by suitable design of conditions and of great practical importance. For example, from a great number of experimental psychological experiments it can be assumed, that people can be made to do anything they are capable of, when the according social condition can be created."

Advertising often uses stereotype gender specific roles of men and women reinforcing existing clichés and it has been criticized as "inadvertently or even intentionally promoting sexism, racism, and ageism... At very least, advertising often reinforces stereotypes by drawing on recognizable "types" in order to tell stories in a single image or 30 second time frame." Activities are depicted as typical male or female (stereotyping). In addition people are reduced to their sexuality or equated with commodities and gender specific qualities are exaggerated. Sexualised female bodies, but increasingly also males, serve as eye-catchers.

In advertising it is usually a woman being depicted as.

(1) a sexual or emotional play toy for the self-affirmation of men

(2) servants of men and children that react to the

demands and complaints of their loved ones with a bad conscience and the promise for immediate improvement (wash, food)

(3) a technically totally clueless being that can only manage a childproof operation

(4) doing ground-work for others, e. g. serving coffee while a journalist interviews a politician

(5) female expert, but stereotype from the fields of fashion, cosmetics, food or at the most, medicine

Thus a great part of advertising is the promotion of products dealing with the appearance of people, mainly for women (in the past almost only for women). Thus, the media put girls and women under high pressure to compare themselves with a propagated ideal beauty. The children's market, where resistance to advertising is weakest, is the "pioneer for ad creep". "Kids are among the most sophisticated observers of ads. They can sing the jingles and identify the logos, and they often have strong feelings about products. What they generally don't understand, however, are the issues that underlie how advertising works.

Mass media are used not only to sell goods but also ideas: how we should behave, what rules are important, who we should respect and what we should value." Youth is increasingly reduced to the role of a consumer. Not only the makers of toys, sweets, ice cream, breakfast food and sport articles prefer to aim their promotion at children and adolescents. For example, an ad for a breakfast cereal on a channel aimed at adults will have music that is a soft ballad, whereas on a channel aimed at children, the same ad will use a catchy rock jingle of the same song to aim at kids. Advertising for other products preferably uses media with which they can also reach the next generation of consumers. "Key advertising messages exploit the emerging independence of young people". Cigarettes, for example, "are used as a fashion accessory and appeal to young women. Other influences on young people include the linking of sporting heroes and smoking through sports sponsorship, the use of cigarettes by popular characters in television programmes and cigarette promotions.

Research suggests that young people are aware of the most heavily advertised cigarette brands." "Product placements show up everywhere, and children aren't exempt. Far from it. The animated film, Foodfight, had 'thousands of products and character icons from the familiar (items) in a grocery store.' Children's books also feature branded items and characters, and millions of them have snack foods as lead characters." Business is interested in children and adolescents because of their buying power and because of their influence on the shopping habits of their parents. As they are easier to influence they are especially targeted by the advertising business. "The marketing industry is facing increased pressure over claimed links between exposure to food advertising and a range of social problems, especially growing obesity levels."

Kids will carry forward brand expectations, whether positive, negative or indifferent Kids are already accustomed to being catered to as consumers. The long term prize: Loyalty of the kid translates into a brand loyal adult customer." The average Canadian child sees 350,000 TV commercials before graduating from high school, spends nearly as much time watching TV as attending classes. In 1980 the Canadian province of Québec banned advertising for children under age 13. "In upholding the consititutional validity of the Quebec Consumer Protection Act restrictions on advertising to children under age 13 (in the case of a challenge by a toy company) the Court held: '...advertising directed at young children is per se manipulative. Such advertising aims to promote products by convincing those who will always believe.'"

Norway (ads directed at children under age 12), and Sweden (television ads aimed at children under age 12) also have legislated broad bans on advertising to children, during child programmes any kind of advertising is forbidden in Sweden, Denmark, Austria and Flemish Belgium. In Greece there is no advertising for kids products from 7 to 22 h. An attempt to restrict advertising directed at children in the USA failed with reference to the First Amendment. In Spain bans are also considered undemocratic. According to critics, the total commercialization of all fields of society, the privatization of public space, the acceleration of consumption and waste of resources including the negative influence on lifestyles and on the environment has not been noticed to the necessary extent. The "hyper-commercialization of the culture is recognized and roundly detested by the citizenry, although the topic scarcely receives a whiff of attention in the media or political culture". "The greatest damage done by advertising is precisely that it incessantly demonstrates the prostitution of men and women who lend their intellects, their voices, their artistic skills to purposes in which they themselves do not believe, and .... that it helps to shatter and ultimately destroy our most precious non-material possessions: the confidence in the existence of meaningful purposes of human activity and respect for the integrity of man."

"The struggle against advertising is therefore essential if we are to overcome the pervasive alienation from all genuine human needs that currently plays such a corrosive role in our society. But in resisting this type of hypercommercialism we should not be under any illusions. Advertising may seem at times to be an almost trivial of omnipresent aspect of our economic system. Yet, as economist A. C. Pigou pointed out, it could only be 'removed altogether' if 'conditions of monopolistic competition' inherent to corporate capitalism were removed. To resist it is to resist the inner logic of capitalism itself, of which it is the pure expression." "Visual pollution, much of it in the form of advertising, is an issue in all the world's large cities. But what is pollution to some is a vibrant part of a city's fabric to others. New York City without Times Square's huge digital billboards or Tokyo without the Ginza's commercial panorama is unthinkable.

Piccadilly Circus would be just a London roundabout without its signage. Still, other cities, like Moscow, have reached their limit and have begun to crack down on over-the-top outdoor advertising." "Many communities have chosen to regulate billboards to protect and enhance their scenic character. The following is by no means a complete list of such communities, but it does give a good idea of the geographic diversity of cities, counties and states that prohibit new construction of billboards. Scenic America estimates the nationwide total of cities and communities prohibiting the construction of new billboards to be at least 1500.

Further technical appliances, such as Spam filters, TV-Zappers, Ad-Blockers for TV's and stickers on mail boxes: "No Advertising" and an increasing number of court cases indicate a growing interest of people to restrict or rid themselves of unwelcome advertising. Consumer protection associations, environment protection groups, globalization opponents, consumption critics, sociologists, media critics, scientists and many others deal with the negative aspects of advertising. "Antipub" in France, "subvertising", culture jamming and adbusting have become established terms in the anti-advertising community.

On the international level globalization critics such as Naomi Klein and Noam Chomsky are also renown media and advertising critics. These groups criticize the complete occupation of public spaces, surfaces, the airwaves, the media, schools etc. and the constant exposure of almost all senses to advertising messages, the invasion of privacy, and that only few consumers are aware that they themselves are bearing the costs for this to the very last penny. Some of these groups, such as the 'The Billboard Liberation Front Creative Group' in San Francisco or Adbusters in Vancouver, Canada, have manifestos. Grassroots organizations campaign against advertising or certain aspects of it in various forms and strategies and quite often have different roots. Adbusters, for example contests and challenges the intended meanings of advertising by subverting them and creating unintended meanings instead. Other groups, like 'Illegal Signs Canada' try to stem the flood of billboards by detecting and reporting ones that have been put up without permit. Examples for various groups and organizations in different countries are 'L'association Résistance à l'Agression Publicitaire' in France, where also media critic Jean Baudrillard is a renown author. The 'Anti Advertising Agency' works with parody and humour to raise awareness about advertising. and 'Commercial Alert' campaigns for the protection of children, family values, community, environmental integrity and democracy.

Media literacy organisations aim at training people, especially children in the workings of the media and advertising in their programmes. In the U. S., for example, the 'Media Education Foundation' produces and distributes documentary films and other educational resources.

'MediaWatch', a Canadian non-profit women's organization works to educate consumers about how they can register their concerns with advertisers and regulators. The Canadian 'Media Awareness Network/Réseau éducation médias' offers one of the world's most comprehensive collections of media education and Internet literacy resources. Its member organizations represent the public, non-profit but also private sectors. Although it stresses its independence it accepts financial support from Bell Canada, CTVGlobeMedia, CanWest, TELUS and S-VOX.

To counter the increasing criticism of advertising aiming at children media literacy organizations are also initiated and funded by corporations and the advertising business themselves. In the U. S. the 'The Advertising Educational Foundation' was created in 1983 supported by ad agencies, advertisers and media companies. It is the advertising industry's provider and distributor of educational content to enrich the understanding of advertising and its role in culture, society and the economy"

Public interest groups suggest that "access to the mental space targeted by advertisers should be taxed, in that at the present moment that space is being freely taken advantage of by advertisers with no compensation paid to the members of the public who are thus being intruded upon. This kind of tax would be a Pigovian tax in that it would act to reduce what is now increasingly seen as a public nuisance.

Efforts to that end are gathering more momentum, with Arkansas and Maine considering bills to implement such a taxation. Florida enacted such a tax in 1987 but was forced to repeal it after six months, as a result of a concerted effort by national commercial interests, which withdrew planned conventions, causing major losses to the tourism industry, and cancelled advertising, causing a loss of 12 million dollars to the broadcast industry alone". In the U. S., for example, advertising is tax deductible and suggestions for possible limits to the advertising tax deduction are met with fierce opposition from the business sector, not to mention suggestions for a special taxation. In other countries, advertising at least is taxed in the same manner services are taxed and in some advertising is subject to special taxation although on a very low level. In many cases the taxation refers especially to media with advertising Austria, Italy, Greece, Netherlands, Turkey, Estonia).

Generally, in the US many communities believe that many forms of outdoor advertising blight the public realm. As long ago as the 1960s in the US there were attempts to ban billboard advertising in the open countryside. Cities such as São Paulo have introduced an outright ban with London also having specific legislation to control unlawful displays. There have been increasing efforts to protect the public interest by regulating the content and the influence of advertising. Some examples are: the ban on television tobacco advertising imposed in many countries, and the total ban of advertising to children under 12 imposed by the Swedish government in 1991.

Though that regulation continues in effect for broadcasts originating within the country, it has been weakened by the European Court of Justice, which had found that Sweden was obliged to accept foreign programming, including those from neighboring countries or via satellite. In Europe and elsewhere, there is a vigorous debate on whether (or how much) advertising to children should be regulated. This debate was exacerbated by a report released by the Kaiser Family Foundation in February 2004 which suggested that food advertising, such as that for fast foods, targeting children was an important factor in the epidemic of childhood obesity in the United States. In many countries - namely New Zealand, South Africa, Canada, and many European countries - the advertising industry operates a system of self-regulation. Advertisers, advertising agencies and the media agree on a code of advertising standards that they attempt to uphold.

The general aim of such codes is to ensure that any advertising is 'legal, decent, honest and truthful'. Some self-regulatory organizations are funded by the industry, but remain independent, with the intent of upholding the standards or codes like the Advertising Standards Authority in the UK. In the UK most forms of outdoor advertising such as the display of billboards is regulated by the UK Town and County Planning system. Currently the display of an advertisement without consent from the Planning Authority is a criminal offense liable to a fine of £2,500 per offence. All of the major outdoor billboard companies in the UK have convictions of this nature. Naturally, many advertisers view governmental regulation or even self-regulation as intrusion of their freedom of speech or a necessary evil. Therefore, they employ a wide-variety of linguistic devices to bypass regulatory laws (e.g. printing English words in bold and French translations in fine print to deal with the Article 120 of the 1994 Toubon Law limiting the use of English in French advertising). The advertisement of controversial products such as cigarettes and condoms is subject to government regulation in many countries. For instance, the tobacco industry is required by law in most countries to display warnings cautioning consumers about the health hazards of their products.

As we have seen, Advertising has gone through five major stages of development: domestic, export, international, multi-national, and global. For global advertisers, there are four, potentially competing, business objectives that must be balanced when developing worldwide advertising: building a brand while speaking with one voice, developing economies of scale in the creative process, maximising local effectiveness of ads, and increasing the company's speed of implementation. Born from the evolutionary stages of global marketing are the three primary and fundamentally different approaches to the development of global advertising executions: exporting executions, producing local executions, and importing ideas that travel. Advertising research is key to determining the success of an ad in any country or region.

The ability to identify which elements and/or moments of an ad that contributes to its success is how economies of scale are maximised. Once one knows what works in an ad, that idea or ideas can be imported by any other market. Market research measures, such as Flow of Attention, Flow of Emotion and branding moments provide insight into what is working in an ad in any country or region because the measures are based on the visual, not verbal, elements of the ad. With the dawn of the Internet came many new advertising opportunities. Popup, Flash, banner, Popunder, advergaming, and email advertisements (the last often being a form of spam) are now commonplace.

The ability to record shows on digital video recorders (such as TiVo) allow users to record the programs for later viewing, enabling them to fast forward through commercials. Additionally, as more seasons of pre-recorded box sets are offered for sale of television programs; fewer people watch the shows on TV.

However, the fact that these sets are sold, means the company will receive additional profits from the sales of these sets. To counter this effect, many advertisers have opted for product placement on TV shows like Survivor. Particularly since the rise of "entertaining" advertising, some people may like an advertisement enough to wish to watch it later or show a friend. In general, the advertising community has not yet made this easy, although some have used the Internet to widely distribute their ads to anyone willing to see or hear them. Another significant trend regarding future of advertising is the growing importance of the niche market using niche or targeted ads. Also brought about by the Internet and the theory of The Long Tail, advertisers will have an increasing ability to reach specific audiences.

In the past, the most efficient way to deliver a message was to blanket the largest mass market audience possible. However, usage tracking, customer profiles and the growing popularity of niche content brought about by everything from blogs to social networking sites, provide advertisers with audiences that are smaller but much better defined, leading to ads that are more relevant to viewers and more effective for companies' marketing products.

Among others, Comcast Spotlight is one such advertiser employing this method in their video on demand menus. These advertisements are targeted to a specific group and can be viewed by anyone wishing to find out more about a particular business or practice at any time, right from their home. This causes the viewer to become proactive and actually choose what advertisements they want to see.

Thus in the realm of advertising agencies, continued industry diversification has seen observers note that "big global clients don't need big global agencies any more". This trend is reflected by the growth of non-traditional agencies in various global markets, such as Canadian business TAXI and SMART in Australia and has been referred to as "a revolution in the ad world".

From the above discussion it becomes obvious that advertisement has become a strong vehicle of disseminating information to the wider range of media audiences. But it has some bad impacts also on the viewers.

REFERENCES

Eskilson, Stephen J. (2007). *Graphic Design: A New History*. New Haven, Connecticut: Yale University Press. p. 58.

McChesney, Robert, *Educators and the Battle for Control of U.S. Broadcasting, 1928-35*, Rich Media, Poor Democracy,

4

Mass Media & Media Bias

> "The word prejudice originally was neutral. It meant judgement formed beforehand, which might be favourable of unfavourable. Yet so predominantly do men form harsh judgements before knowledge, that prejudice came to mean injurious."
>
> —*Marshall Wingfield*

As is generally observed everywhere mass media do not act as a neutral mode. Bias or prejudice is found in varying degrees. In fact to uphold impartiality in media action is a great task to accomplish. Here in the present chapter we will elucidate media bias, its nature, magnitude and impact on the society.

In common parlance, Media bias refers to the real and perceived bias of journalists and news producers within the mass media, in the selection of which events and stories are reported and how they are covered. The term "media bias" usually implies a pervasive or widespread bias contravening the standards of journalism, rather than the perspective of an individual journalist or article. The direction and degree of media bias in various countries is widely disputed, although its causes are both practical and theoretical. Practical limitations to media neutrality include the inability of journalists to report all available stories and facts, and the requirement that selected facts be linked into a coherent narrative (Newton 1989).

Since it is impossible to report everything, some selectivity is inevitable. Government influence, including overt and covert censorship, biases the media in some countries. Market forces that can result in a biased presentation include the ownership of the news source, the selection of staff, the preferences of an intended audience, pressure from advertisers, or reduced funding due to lower ratings or governmental funding cuts. Political affiliations arise from ideological positions of media owners and journalists.

The space or air time available for reports, as well as deadlines needing to be met, can lead to incomplete and apparently biased stories. Political bias has been a feature of the mass media since its birth with the invention of the printing press. The expense of early printing equipment restricted media production to a limited number of people. Historians have found that publishers often served the interests of powerful social groups.

Remarkably, in the nineteenth century, journalists began to recognize the concept of unbiased reporting as an integral part of journalistic ethics. This coincided with the rise of journalism as a powerful social force. Even today, though, the most conscientiously objective journalists cannot avoid accusations of bias. Like newspapers, the broadcast media (radio and television) have been used as a mechanism for propaganda from their earliest days, a tendency made more pronounced by the initial ownership of broadcast spectrum by national governments.

Although a process of media deregulation has placed the majority of the western broadcast media in private hands, there still exists a strong government presence, or even monopoly, in the broadcast media of many countries across the globe. At the same time, the concentration of media in private hands, and frequently amongst a comparatively small number of individuals, has also lead to accusations of media bias. There are many examples of accusations of bias being used as a political tool, sometimes resulting in government censorship.

In the United States, in 1798, Congress passed the Alien and Sedition Acts, which prohibited newspapers from publishing "false, scandalous, or malicious writing" against the government, including any public opposition to any law or presidential act. This act was in effect until 1801. During the American Civil War, President Abraham Lincoln accused newspapers in the border states of bias in favor of the Southern cause, and ordered many newspapers closed. Chancellor Adolf Hitler of Germany, in the years leading up to World War II, accused newspapers of Marxist bias, an accusation echoed by pro-German media in England and the United States.

Generally, politicians who favored the United States entering World War II on the German side asserted that the international media were controlled by Jews, and that reports of German mistreatment of Jews were biased and without foundation. Hollywood was said to be a hotbed of Jewish bias, and films such as Charlie Chaplin's The Great Dictator were offered as proof. In the 1980s, the South African government accused newspapers of liberal bias and instituted government censorship. In 1989, the newspaper *New Nation* was closed by the government for three months for publishing anti-apartheid propaganda. Other newspapers were not closed, but were extensively censored.

Some published the censored sections blacked out, to

demonstrate the extent of government censorship. In the USA during the labor union movement and the civil rights movement, newspapers supporting liberal social reform were accused by conservative newspapers of communist bias. Film and television media were accused of bias in favor of mixing of the races, and many television programs with racially mixed casts, such as *I Spy* and *Star Trek*, were not aired on Southern stations.

Notably, during the war between the United States and North Vietnam, Vice President Spiro Agnew accused newspapers of anti-American bias, and in a famous speech delivered in San Diego in 1970, called anti-war protesters "The nattering nabobs of negativism." Not all accusations of bias are political. Science writer Martin Gardner has accused the entertainment media of anti-science bias. He claims that television programs such as *The X-Files* promote superstition. In contrast, the Competitive Enterprise Institute accuses the media of being biased in favor of science and against business interests, and of credulously reporting science that purports to show that greenhouse gasses cause global warming.

Categorisation

(1) Advertising bias, corporate media depends on advertising revenue for funding. This relationship promotes a bias to please the advertisers.

(2) "Accidental bias" which could include errors and misinformation (re: expediency) or editors accidentally reinterpreting a reporter's work.

(3) Corporate bias, coverage' of political campaigns in such a way as to favor or oppose corporate interests, and the reporting of issues to favor the interests of the owners of the news media or its advertisers. Some critics view the

financing of news outlets through advertisers as an inherent bias.

(4) Ethnic or racial bias, including racism, nationalism.

(5) Class bias, including bias favoring one social class and bias ignoring (or exaggerating) social or class divisions.

(6) Political bias, including bias in favor of or against a particular political party, candidate, or policy. Other complaints are: the American media has an "either or" view by only focusing on Democrats or Republicans, and ignoring other lines of thought such as socialism and libertarianism.

(7) Religious and cultural bias, including bias in which one religious or nonreligious viewpoint is given preference over others.

(8) Mainstream bias, a tendency to report what everyone else is reporting, and to gather news from a relatively small number of easily available sources.

(9) Sensationalism, bias in favor of the exceptional over the ordinary. This includes the practice whereby exceptional news may be overemphasized, distorted or fabricated to boost commercial ratings; entertainment news is often subjected to sensationalism.

(10) Bias based on sex, age, background, education, language, among others. (For instance woman's issues are rarely featured in mainstream news, and a poorly written letter won't make it into the Letters to the Editor section.)

(11) Exaggerated influence of minority views: Like sensationalism, this is a tendency to emphasize the new and the different over the *status quo* or existing consensus. This may be done in an attempt to be "fair", or to find something worth reporting.

(12) Bias toward ease or expediency: This can be a tendency to present information which is already widely reported in other news media, i.e. "jumping on the bandwagon" or "following the leader", presentation of "fluff pieces" which are of questionable journalistic merit (such as coverage in news media of the personal lives of celebrities, or "news you can use"-style reporting which offers consumer advice which is widely viewed as common sense), and over representation of crime reporting, particularly street crime. This type of bias is largely attributed to the relatively low cost of presenting these stories (compared to investigative journalism which tends to require more time and research, and thus more money, to produce), competition between commercial news media for consumers, ratings and ad revenue, and a 24-hour news cycle which demands constant output.

Here it is worth mentioning that valid questions remain about media performance and the role of public communications practitioners in coercing perception and judgement. There are some researchers who use a "social construction of reality" framework to analyze media and the ways in which information is filtered. According to scholar Richard Alan Nelson's (2003) study *Tracking Propaganda to the Source: Tools for Analyzing Media Bias*, media effects findings suggest that when bias occurs it stems from a combination of ten factors:

(a) Framing devices are employed in stories by featuring some angles and downplaying others.

(b) The media are neither objective nor completely honest in their portrayal of important issues.

(c) The news is a product not only of deliberate manipulation, but of the ideological and economic conditions under which the media operate.

(d) While appearing independent, the news media are institutions that are controlled or heavily influenced by government and business interests experienced with manufacturing of consent/consensus.

(e) Reporters' sources frequently dominate the flow of information as a way of furthering their own overt and hidden agendas. In particular, the heavy reliance on political officials and other-government related experts occurs through a preferential sourcing selection process which excludes dissident voices.

(f) Citizens must avoid self-censorship by reading divergent sources and maintaining a critical perspective on the media in order to make informed choices and participate effectively in the public policy process.

(g) Journalists widely accept the faulty premise that the government's collective intentions are benevolent, despite occasional mistakes.

(h) The regular use of the word "we" by journalists in referring to their government's actions implies nationalistic complicity with those policies.

(i) There is an absence of historical context and contemporary comparisons in reportage which would make news more meaningful.

(j) The failure to provide follow up assessment is further evidence of a pack journalism mentality that at the conclusion of a "feeding frenzy" wants to move on to other stories.

Currently, Media bias is studied at schools of journalism, university departments (including Media studies, Cultural studies and Peace studies) and by many independent watchdog groups from various parts of the political spectrum.

In the United States, many of these studies focus on issues of a conservative/liberal balance in the media. Other focuses include international differences in reporting, as well as bias in reporting of particular issues such as economic class or environmental interests. A widely-cited public opinion study documents a correlation between news source and certain misconceptions about the Iraq war. Conducted by the Program on International Policy Attitudes in October 2003, the poll asked Americans whether they believed statements about the Iraq war that were known to be false. Respondents were also asked which was their primary news source: Fox News, CBS, NBC, ABC, CNN, "Print sources," or NPR.

By cross referencing the responses according to primary news source, the study showed that higher numbers of Fox News watchers held certain misconceptions about the Iraq war. The director of Program on International Policy (PIPA), Stephen Kull said, "While we cannot assert that these misconceptions created the support for going to war with Iraq, it does appear likely that support for the war would be substantially lower if fewer members of the public had these misperceptions." The Glasgow Media Group carried out the Bad News Studies, a series of detailed analyses of television broadcasts (and later newspaper coverage) in the United Kingdom. (Eldridge, 2000).

Published between 1976 and 1985, the Bad News Studies used content analysis, interviews and covert participant observation to conclude that news was biased against trade unions, blaming them for breaking wage negotiating guidelines and causing high inflation. Martin Harrison's *TV News: Whose Bias?* (1985) criticized the methodology of the Glasgow Media Group, arguing that the GMG identified bias selectively, via their own preconceptions about what phrases qualify as biased descriptions. For example, the GMG sees the word "idle" to describe striking workers as pejorative, despite the word being used by strikers themselves.

It is apt to note here that Herman and Chomsky (1988) proposed a propaganda model hypothesizing systematic biases of U.S. media from structural economic causes. They hypothesize media ownership by corporations, funding from advertising, the use of official sources, efforts to discredit independent media ("flak"), and "anti-communist" ideology as the filters that bias news in favor of U.S. corporate interests. Their propaganda model first and foremost disuses self censorship through the corporate system (see corporate censorship); that reporters and especially editors share and/or acquire values with corporate elites in order to further their careers.

Those that don't are usually weeded out or marginalized. Such examples have been dramatized in fact based movie dramas as "Good Night, and Good Luck" and "The Insider" or demonstrated in the documentary "The Corporation". George Orwell originally wrote a preface for his book "Animal Farm", which focuses on British self censorship. "The sinister fact about literary censorship in England is that it is largely voluntary. ... [Things are] kept right out of the British press, not because the Government intervened but because of a general tacit agreement that 'it wouldn't do' to mention that particular fact." As if to prove the point, the preface itself was censored and is not published with most copies of the book. The academic study cited most frequently by critics of a "liberal media bias" in American journalism is *The Media Elite,* a 1986 book co-authored by political scientists Robert Lichter, Stanley Rothman, and Linda Lichter.

They surveyed journalists at national media outlets

such as the New York Times, Washington Post, and the broadcast networks. The survey found that most of these journalists were Democratic voters whose attitudes were well to the left of the general public on a variety of topics, including such hot-button social issues such as abortion, affirmative action, and gay rights. Then they compared journalists' attitudes to their coverage of controversial issues such as the safety of nuclear power, school busing to promote racial integration, and the energy crisis of the 1970s. The book's most thorough case study involved nuclear energy.

The survey of journalists showed that most were highly skeptical about nuclear safety. However, the authors conducted a separate survey of scientists in energy related fields, who were much more sanguine about nuclear safety issues. They then conducted a content analysis of nuclear energy coverage in the media outlets they had surveyed. They found that the opinions of sources who were cited as scientific experts reflected the antinuclear sentiments of journalists, rather than the more pro-nuclear perspectives held by most energy scientists. The authors concluded that journalists' coverage of controversial issues reflected their own attitudes, and the predominance of political liberals in newsrooms therefore pushed news coverage in a liberal direction.

They presented this tilt as a mostly unconscious process of like-minded individuals projecting their shared assumptions onto their interpretations of reality. At the time the study was embraced mainly by conservative columnists and politicians, who adopted the findings as scientific proof of liberal media bias. Many of the positions in the preceding study are supported by a 2002 study by Jim A. Kuypers: Press Bias and Politics: How the Media Frame Controversial Issues. In this study of 116 mainstream

US papers (including *The New York Times*, the *Washington Post, Los Angeles Times,* and the *San Francisco Chronicle*), Kuypers found that the mainstream print press in America operate within a narrow range of liberal beliefs. Those who expressed points of view further to the left were generally ignored, whereas those who expressed moderate or conservative points of view were often actively denigrated or labeled as holding a minority point of view. In short, if a political leader, regardless of party, spoke within the press-supported range of acceptable discourse, he or she would receive positive press coverage.

If a politician, again regardless of party, were to speak outside of this range, he or she would receive negative press or be ignored. Kuypers also found that the liberal points of view expressed in editorial and opinion pages were found in hard news coverage of the same issues. Although focusing primarily on the issues of race and homosexuality, Kuypers found that the press injected opinion into its news coverage of other issues such as welfare reform, environmental protection, and gun control; in all cases favoring a liberal point of view. Studies reporting perceptions of liberal bias in the media are not limited to studies of print media.

A joint study by the Joan Shorenstein Center on Press, Politics and Public Policy at Harvard University and the Project for Excellence in Journalism found that people see liberal media bias in television news media such as CNN. Although both CNN and Fox were perceived in the study as being left of center, CNN was perceived as being more liberal than Fox. Moreover, the study's findings concerning CNN's perceived liberal bias are echoed in other studies. There is also a growing economics literature on mass media bias, both on the theoretical and the empirical side.

On the theoretical side the focus is on understanding to what extent the political positioning of mass media outlets is mainly driven by demand or supply factors. Tim Groseclose of UCLA and Jeff Milyo of the University of Missouri at Columbia use think tank quotes, in order to estimate the relative position of mass media outlets in the political spectrum. The idea is to trace out which think tanks are quoted by various mass media outlets within news stories, and to match these think tanks with the political position of members of the U.S. Congress who quote them in a non-negative way. Using this procedure, Groseclose and Milyo obtain the stark result that all sampled news providers - except Fox News' Special Report and the Washington Times- are located to the left of the average Congress member, i.e. there are signs of a liberal bias in the US news media.

However, the news media also show a remarkable degree of centrism, just because all outlets but one are located from an ideological point of view between the average Democrat and average Republican in Congress. The methods Groseclose and Milyo used to calculate this bias have been criticized by Mark Liberman, a professor of Computer Science at the University of Pennsylvania. Liberman concludes by saying he thinks "that many if not most of the complaints directed against G&M are motivated in part by ideological disagreement — just as much of the praise for their work is motivated by ideological agreement.

It would be nice if there were a less politically fraught body of data on which such modeling exercises could be explored." Sendhil Mullainathan and Andrei Shleifer of Harvard University construct a behavioural model, which is built around the assumption that readers and viewers hold beliefs that they would like to see confirmed by news providers. When news customers share common beliefs, profit-maximizing media outlets find it optimal to select and/or frame stories in order to pander to those beliefs.

On the other hand, when beliefs are heterogeneous, news providers differentiate their offer and segment the market, by providing news stories that are slanted towards the two extreme positions in the spectrum of beliefs. John Lott and Kevin Hassett of the American Enterprise Institute study the coverage of economic news by looking at a panel of 389 U.S. newspapers from 1991 to 2004, and from 1985 to 2004 for a subsample comprising the top 10 newspapers and the Associated Press. For each release of official data about a set of economic indicators, the authors analyze how newspapers decide to report on them, as reflected by the tone of the related headlines.

The idea is to check whether newspapers display some kind of partisan bias, by giving more positive or negative coverage to the same economic figure, as a function of the political affiliation of the incumbent President. Controlling for the economic data being released, the authors find that there are between 9.6 and 14.7 percent fewer positive stories when the incumbent President is a Republican. Steve Ansolabehere, Rebecca Lessem and Jim Snyder of the Massachusetts Institute of Technology analyze the political orientation of endorsements by U.S. newspapers.

They find an upward trend in the average propensity to endorse a candidate, and in particular an incumbent one. There are also some changes in the average ideological slant of endorsements: while in the 40s and in the 50s there was a clear advantage to Republican candidates, this advantage continuously eroded in subsequent decades, to the extent that in the 90s the authors find a slight Democratic lead in the average endorsement choice. Riccardo Puglisi of the Massachusetts Institute of Technology looks at the editorial choices of the *New York Times* from 1946 to 1997. He finds that the *Times* displays Democratic partisanship, with some watchdog aspects. This is the case, because during presidential campaigns the Times systematically gives more coverage to Democratic topics of civil rights, health care, labor and social welfare, but only when the incumbent president is a Republican. These topics are classified as Democratic ones, because Gallup polls show that on average U.S. citizens think that Democratic candidates would be better at handling problems related to them.

According to Puglisi, in the post-1960 period the Times displays a more symmetric type of watchdog behaviour, just because during presidential campaigns it also gives more coverage to the typically Republican issue of Defense when the incumbent President is a Democrat, and less so when the incumbent is a Republican. Alan Gerber and Dean Karlan of Yale University use an experimental approach to examine not whether the media are biased, but whether the media influence political decisions and attitudes. They conduct a randomized control trial just prior to the November 2005 gubernatorial election in Virginia and randomly assign individuals in Northern Virginia to (a) a treatment group that receives a free subscription to the Washington Post, (b) a treatment group that receives a free subscription to the Washington Times, or (c) a control group. They find that those who are assigned to the Washington Post treatment group are eight percentage points more likely to vote for the Democrat in the elections. The report also found that "exposure to either newspaper was weakly linked to a movement away from the Bush administration and Republicans." Another unaffiliated group, Media Study Group, established seven categories of poor journalistic practice: for example, the journalist stating personal opinion in a report, asserting incorrect facts, applying unequal space or treatment to two sides of a controversial issue; then analyzed *The Age Newspaper* (Melbourne Australia) for the frequency of infraction of this code of practice. The resultant instances were then analyzed statistically with respect to the frequency they supported one or other side of the two-sided controversial issue under consideration.

Evaluation of Media Bias

Richard Alan Nelson's (2003) study cited above on *Tracking Propaganda to the Source: Tools for Analyzing Media Bias* reports there are at least 12 methods used to analyze the existence of and quantify bias:

1. Surveys of the political/cultural attitudes of journalists, particularly members of the media elite, and of journalism students.
2. Studies of journalists' previous professional connections.
3. Collections of quotations in which prominent journalists reveal their beliefs about politics and/or the proper role of their profession.
4. Computer word-use and topic analysis searches to determine content and labeling.
5. Studies of policies recommended in news stories.
6. Comparisons of the agenda of the news and entertainment media with agendas of political candidates or other activists.
7. Positive/negative coverage analysis.
8. Reviews of the personal demographics of media decision makers.

9. Comparisons of advertising sources/content which influence information/entertainment content.
10. Analyses of the extent of government propaganda and public relations (PR) industry impact on media.
11. Studies of the use of experts and spokespersons etc. by media vs. those not selected to determine the interest groups and ideologies represented vs. those excluded.
12. Research into payments of journalists by corporations and trade associations to speak before their groups and the impact that may have on coverage.

How to Avoid

In fact, a technique used to avoid bias is the "point/counterpoint" or "round table," an adversarial format in which representatives of opposing views comment on an issue. This approach theoretically allows diverse views to appear in the media. However, the person organizing the report still has the responsibility to choose people who really represent the breadth of opinion, to ask them non-prejudicial questions, and to edit or arbitrate their comments fairly. When done carelessly, a point/counterpoint can be as unfair as a simple biased report, by suggesting that the "losing" side lost on its merits.

The Skeptics Society has accused reporters of misusing the point/counterpoint format by giving more time to superstitions than to their scientific rebuttals. Using this format can also lead to accusations that the reporter has created a misleading appearance that viewpoints have equal validity (sometimes called "false balance". This may happen when a taboo exists around one of the viewpoints, or when one of the representatives habitually makes claims that are easily shown to be inaccurate.

One such allegation of misleading balance came from Mark Halperin, political director of ABC News. He stated in an internal e-mail message that reporters should not "artificially hold [George W. Bush and John Kerry 'equally' accountable" to the public interest, and that complaints from Bush supporters were an attempt to "get away with ... renewed efforts to win the election by destroying Senator Kerry." When the Drudge Report published this message, many Bush supporters viewed it as "smoking gun" evidence that Halperin was using ABC to propagandize against Bush to Kerry's benefit, by interfering with reporters' attempts to avoid bias.

An academic content analysis of election news later found that coverage at ABC, CBS, and NBC was more favorable toward Kerry than Bush, while coverage at Fox News Channel was more favorable toward Bush. Scott Norvell, the London bureau chief for Fox News, stated in a May 20, 2005 interview with the Wall Street Journal that "Even we at Fox News manage to get some lefties on the air occasionally, and often let them finish their sentences before we club them to death and feed the scraps to Karl Rove and Bill O'Reilly.

And those who hate us can take solace in the fact that they aren't subsidizing Bill's bombast; we payers of the BBC license fee don't enjoy that peace of mind. Fox News is, after all, a private channel and our presenters are quite open about where they stand on particular stories. That's our appeal. People watch us because they know what they are getting. The Beeb's (British Broadcasting Corporation) (BBC) institutionalized leftism would be easier to tolerate if the corporation was a little more honest about it". Another technique used to avoid bias is disclosure of affiliations that may be considered a possible conflict of interest. This is especially apparent when a news organization is reporting a story with some relevancy to the news organization itself or to its ownership individuals or conglomerate. Often this disclosure is mandated by the laws or regulations pertaining to stocks and securities.

Commentators on news stories involving stocks are often required to disclose any ownership interest in those corporations or in its competitors. In rare cases, a news organization may dismiss or reassign staff members who appear biased. This approach was used in the Killian documents affair and after Peter Arnett's interview with the Iraqi press. This approach is presumed to have been employed in the case of Dan Rather over a heavily biased story that he ran on 60 Minutes in the month prior to the 2004 election that attempted to impugn the military record of George W. Bush by relying on obviously fake documents that were provided by a Democrat Party operative.

Finally, some countries have laws enforcing balance in state-owned media. Since 1991, the CBC and Radio Canada, its Francophone counterpart, are governed by the Broadcasting Act. This act states, amongst other things: the programming provided by the Canadian broadcasting system should (i) be varied and comprehensive, providing a balance of information, enlightenment and entertainment for men, women and children of all ages, interests and tastes, (...) (iv) provide a reasonable opportunity for the public to be exposed to the expression of differing views on matters of public concern.

Mass media, despite its ability to project worldwide, is limited in its cross-ethnic compatibility by one simple attribute - language. Ethnicity, being largely developed by a divergence in geography, language, culture, genes and similarly, point of view, has the potential to be countered by a common source of information. Therefore, language, in the absence of translation, comprises a barrier to a worldwide community of debate and opinion, although it is also true that media within any given society may be split along class, political or regional lines.

Furthermore, if the language is translated, the translator has room to shift a bias by choosing weighed words for translation. Language may also be seen as a political factor in mass media, particularly in instances where a society is characterized by a large number of languages spoken by its populace. The choice of language of mass media may represent a bias towards the group most likely to speak that language, and can limit the public participation by those who do not speak the language. On the other hand, there have also been attempts to use a common-language mass media to reach out to a large, geographically dispersed population, such as in the use of Arabic language by news channel Al Jazeera. Many media theorists concerned with language and media bias point towards the media of the United States, a large country where English is spoken by the vast majority of the population. Some theorists argue that the common language is not homogenizing; and that there still remain strong differences expressed within the mass media.

This viewpoint asserts that moderate views are bolstered by drawing influences from the extremes of the political spectrum. In the United States, the national news therefore contributes to a sense of cohesion within the society, proceeding from a similarly informed population. According to this model, most views within society are freely expressed, and the mass media are accountable to the people and tends to reflect the spectrum of opinion. Language may also be a more subtle form of bias. Use of a word with positive or negative connotations rather than a more neutral synonym can form a biased picture in the audience's mind. It makes a difference whether the media calls a group "terrorist" or "freedom fighters" or "insurgents".

Many news organizations reflect or are perceived to reflect in some way the viewpoint of the geographic, ethnic, and national population that they primarily serve. Media within countries is sometimes seen as being sycophantic or unquestioning about the country's government. Western media are often criticized in the rest of the world (including eastern Europe, Asia, Africa, and the Middle East) as being pro-Western with regard to a variety of political, cultural and economic issues. Al Jazeera has been frequently criticized in the West about its coverage of Arab world issues. The Israeli-Palestinian conflict and wider Arab-Israeli issues are a particularly controversial area, and nearly all coverage of any kind generates accusation of bias from one or both sides.

It has been observed that the world's principal suppliers of news, the news agencies, and the main buyers of news are Anglophone corporations and this gives an Anglophone bias to the selection and depiction of events. Anglophone definitions of what constitutes news are paramount; the news provided originates in Anglophone capitals and responds first to their own rich domestic markets. Despite the plethora of news services, most news printed and broadcast throughout the world each day comes from only a few major agencies, the three largest of which are the Associated Press, Reuters and Agence France-Presse. Although these agencies are 'global' in the sense of their activities, they each retain significant associations with particular nations, namely France (AFP), the United States (AP) and the United Kingdom (Reuters).

Chambers and Tinckell suggest that the so-called global media are agents of Anglophone values which privilege norms of 'competitive individualism, laissez faire capitalism, parliamentary democracy and consumerism.' They see the presentation of the English language as international as a further feature of Anglophone dominance.

It is remembered that Media bias towards religion is most obvious in countries where the media are controlled by the state, which is in turn dominated by a particular religion. In these instances, bias against other faiths can be explicit and virulent. But even in countries with freedom of religion and a free press, the dominant religion exerts some amount of influence on the media. In nations where Christianity is the majority faith, reporters tend to focus on the activities of the Christian community, to the exclusion of other faiths. But the opposite may also occur, with media self-consciously avoiding reporting on any religious matters at all in order to avoid the appearance of favoring one faith over another, or presenting religious faith and phenomenon in a negative light. This type of bias is often seen with reporting on new religious movements. It is often the case that the only view the public gets of a new religious movement, controversial group or purported cult is a negative and sensationalized report by the media.

For example, most new or minority religious movements only receive media coverage when something sensational occurs, e.g. the mass suicide of a cult or illegal activities of a leader in the religious movement. According to the *Encyclopedia of Social Work* (19th edition), the news media play an influential role in the general public's perception of cults. As reported in several studies, the media have depicted cults as problematic, controversial, and threatening from the beginning, tending to favor sensationalistic stories over balanced public debates (Beckford, 1985; Richardson, Best, & Bromley, 1991; Victor, 1993).

It furthers the analysis that media reports on cults rely heavily on police officials and cult "experts" who portray cult activity as dangerous and destructive, and when divergent views are presented, they are often overshadowed by horrific stories of ritualistic torture, sexual abuse, mind control, etc. The apparent bias of media is not always specifically political in nature. The news media tend to appeal to a specific audience, which means that stories that affect a large number of people on a global scale often receive less coverage in some markets than local stories, such as a public school shooting, a celebrity wedding, a plane crash, or similarly glamorous or shocking stories. For example, the deaths of millions of people in an ethnic conflict in Africa might be afforded scant mention in American media, while the shooting of five people in a high school is analyzed in depth.

The reason for this type of bias is a function of what the public wants to watch and/or what producers and publishers believe the public wants to watch. Bias has also been claimed in instances referred to as conflict of interest, whereby the owners of media outlets have vested interests in other commercial enterprises or political parties. In such cases in the United States, the media outlet is required to disclose the conflict of interest.

From the preceding discussion it has become obvious that media bias has both advantages in certain circumstances and disadvantage in certain other. In fact, media should play an importial role in upholding righteousness and making healthing public opinion for the larger benefit of society as a whole.

REFERENCES

Chambers and Tinckell (1998) Angocentric versions of the international: the privileging of Anglo-ethnicity in cultural studies and the global media. 21st conference of IAMCR, Glasgow.

Liberman, Mark (2005-12-23). "Multiplying ideologies considered harmful". Language Log. http://itre.cis.upenn.edu/~myl/languagelog/archives/002724.html.

Robins, Susan P., *Encyclopedia of Social Work, 19th Edition*, National Association of Social Workers. Washington, DC. 1997 Update.

Ronald Bailey, *Global Warming and Other Eco Myths: How the Environmental Movement Uses False Science to Scare Us to Death*, Prima Lifestyles; 2002.

Weatherly, Jeffrey N, et al., "Perceptions of Political Bias in the Headlines of Two Major News Organizations," *The Harvard International Journal of Press / Politics* (2007) (12), 91 at p. 97.

5

World Wide Web (WWW) and Web Browsing

"Never associate with idiots on their own level because, being an intelligent man, you'll try to deal with them on their level- and on their level they'll beat you every time."

—Jean Cocteau

The World Wide Web is the only thing I know of whose shortened form takes three times longer to say than its long form.

—Douglas Adams,
The Independent on Sunday, 1999

As of now, World Wide Web (www) is a popular mode of communication media. In practice it is sometimes shortened, in English usage, to "triple double-you" or run together as "DubaDubaDub-u." In other languages, "www" may be pronounced like "veh-veh-veh". The early "w^3" abbreviation is now defunct.

Basically, World Wide Web (or the "Web") is a system of interlinked, hypertext documents that runs over the Internet. With a Web browser, a user views Web pages that may contain text, images, and other multimedia and navigates between them using hyperlinks. The Web was created around 1990 by the Englishman Tim Berners-Lee and the Belgian Robert Cailliau working at CERN in Geneva, Switzerland. Since then, Berners-Lee has played an active role in guiding the development of Web standards (such as the markup languages in which Web pages are composed), and in recent years has advocated his vision of a Semantic Web.

In fact, the underlying ideas of the Web can be traced as far back as 1980, when, at CERN in Switzerland, the Englishman Tim Berners-Lee built ENQUIRE (referring to *Enquire Within Upon Everything*, a book he recalled from his youth). While it was rather different from the Web in use today, it contained many of the same core ideas (and even some of the ideas of Berners-Lee's next project after the WWW, the Semantic Web). In March 1989, Tim Berners-Lee wrote *Information Management: A Proposal*, which referenced ENQUIRE and described a more elaborate information management system. With help from Robert Cailliau, he published a more formal proposal for the World Wide Web on November 12, 1990. A NeXTcube was used by Berners-Lee as the world's first web server and also to write the first web browser, WorldWideWeb in 1990. By Christmas 1990, Berners-Lee had built all the tools necessary for a working Web: the first Web browser (which was a Web editor as well), the first Web server and the first Web pages which described the project itself. On August 6, 1991, he posted a short summary of the World Wide Web project on the alt.hypertext newsgroup. This date also marked the debut of the Web as a publicly available service on the Internet.

It is pertinent to note here that the crucial underlying concept of hypertext originated with older projects from the 1960s, such as Ted Nelson's Project Xanadu and Douglas Engelbart's oN-Line System (NLS). Both Nelson and

Engelbart were in turn inspired by Vannevar Bush's microfilm-based "memex," which was described in the 1945 essay "As We May Think".

Berners-Lee's breakthrough was to marry hypertext to the Internet. In his book *Weaving The Web,* he explains that he had repeatedly suggested that a marriage between the two technologies was possible to members of *both* technical communities, but when no one took up his invitation, he finally tackled the project himself. In the process, he developed a system of globally unique identifiers for resources on the Web and elsewhere: the Uniform Resource Identifier.

The World Wide Web had a number of differences from other hypertext systems that were then available:

1. The WWW required only unidirectional links rather than bidirectional ones. This made it possible for someone to link to another resource without action by the owner of that resource. It also significantly reduced the difficulty of implementing Web servers and browsers (in comparison to earlier systems), but in turn presented the chronic problem of link rot.
2. Unlike predecessors such as HyperCard, the World Wide Web was non-proprietary, making it possible to develop servers and clients independently and to add extensions without licensing restrictions.

Notably, on April 30, 1993, CERN announced that the World Wide Web would be free to anyone, with no fees due. Coming two months after the announcement that gopher was no longer free to use, this produced a rapid shift away from gopher and towards the Web. An early popular Web browser was ViolaWWW which was based upon HyperCard. Scholars generally agree, however, that the turning point for the World Wide Web began with the introduction of the Mosaic web browser in 1993, a graphical browser developed by a team at the National Center for Supercomputing Applications at the University of Illinois at Urbana-Champaign (NCSA-UIUC), led by Marc Andreessen. Funding for Mosaic came from the *High-Performance Computing and Communications Initiative*, a funding program initiated by then-Senator Al Gore's *High Performance Computing and Communication Act of 1991* also known as the *Gore Bill*. Prior to the release of Mosaic, graphics were not commonly mixed with text in Web pages and its popularity was less than older protocols in use over the Internet, such as Gopher protocol and Wide area information server. Mosaic's graphical user interface allowed the Web to become by far the most popular Internet protocol.

Functioning

Viewing a Web page or other resource on the World Wide Web normally begins either by typing the URL of the page into a Web browser, or by following a hypertext link to that page or resource. The first step, behind the scenes, is for the server-name part of the URL to be resolved into an IP address by the global, distributed Internet database known as the Domain name system or DNS.

The browser then establishes a TCP connection with the server at that IP address. The next step is for an HTTP request to be sent to the Web server, requesting the resource. In the case of a typical Web page, the HTML text is first requested and parsed by the browser, which then makes additional requests for graphics and any other files that form a part of the page in quick succession. When considering web site popularity statistics, these additional file requests give rise to the difference between one single 'page view' and an associated number of server 'hits'. The Web browser then renders the page as described by the HTML, CSS and other files received, incorporating the images and other resources as necessary. This produces the on-screen page that the viewer sees.

Remarkably, most Web pages will themselves contain hyperlinks to other related pages and perhaps to downloads, source documents, definitions and other Web resources. Such a collection of useful, related resources, interconnected via hypertext links, is what has been dubbed a 'web' of information. Making it available on the Internet created what Tim Berners-Lee first called the WorldWideWeb in 1990.

Web Standards

At its core, the Web is made up of three standards:

(a) the *Uniform Resource Identifier* (URI), which is a universal system for referencing resources on the Web, such as Web pages;

(b) the *HyperText Transfer Protocol* (HTTP), which specifies how the browser and server communicate with each other; and

(c) the *HyperText Markup Language* (HTML), used to define the structure and content of hypertext documents.

It is significant to note that Berners-Lee now heads the World Wide Web Consortium (W3C), which develops and maintains these and other standards that enable computers on the Web to effectively store and communicate different forms of information.

Caching

If the user returns to a page fairly soon, it is likely that the data will not be retrieved from the source Web server, as above, again. By default, browsers cache all web resources on the local hard drive. An HTTP request will be sent by the browser that asks for the data *only if it has been updated since the last download*. If it has not, the cached version will be reused in the rendering step.

This is particularly valuable in reducing the amount of Web traffic on the Internet. The decision about expiration is made independently for each resource (image, stylesheet, JavaScript file etc., as well as for the HTML itself).

Thus even on sites with highly dynamic content, many of the basic resources are only supplied once per session or less. It is worth it for any Web site designer to collect all the CSS and JavaScript into a few site-wide files so that they can be downloaded into users' caches and reduce page download times and demands on the server. There are other components of the Internet that can cache Web content. The most common in practice are often built into corporate and academic firewalls where they cache web resources requested by one user for the benefit of all.

Some search engines such as Google or Yahoo! also store cached content from Web sites. Apart from the facilities built into Web servers that can ascertain when physical files have been updated, it is possible for designers of dynamically generated web pages to control the HTTP headers sent back to requesting users, so that pages are not cached when they should not be — for example Internet banking and news pages. This helps with understanding the difference between the HTTP 'GET' and 'POST' verbs—data requested with a GET may be cached, if other conditions are met, whereas data obtained after POSTing information to the server usually will not.

JavaScript and Java

Practically, a significant advance in Web technology was Sun Microsystems' Java platform. It enables Web pages to embed small programs (called applets) directly into the view. These applets run on the end-user's computer, providing a richer user interface than simple web pages. Java client-side applets never gained the popularity that Sun had hoped for, for a variety of reasons including lack of integration with other content (applets were confined to small boxes within the rendered page) and the fact that many computers at the time were supplied to end users without a suitably installed JVM, and so required a download by the user before applets would appear.

Adobe Flash now performs many of the functions that were originally envisioned for Java applets including the playing of video content, animation and some rich UI features. Java itself has become more widely used as a platform and language for server-side and other programming. JavaScript, on the other hand, is a scripting language that was initially developed for use within Web pages. The standardized version is ECMAScript. While its name is similar to Java, JavaScript was developed by Netscape and it has almost nothing to do with Java, apart from that, like Java, its syntax is derived from the C programming language. In conjunction with a Web page's Document Object Model, JavaScript has become a much more powerful technology than its creators originally envisioned. The manipulation of a page's Document Object Model after the page is delivered to the client has been called Dynamic HTML (DHTML), to emphasize a shift away from *static* HTML displays. In its simplest form, all the optional information and actions available on a JavaScripted Web page will have been downloaded when the page was first delivered.

Ajax ("Asynchronous JavaScript And XML") is a JavaScript-based technology that may have a significant effect on the development of the World Wide Web. Ajax provides a method whereby large or small parts *within* a Web page may be updated, using new information obtained over the network in response to user actions. This allows the page to be much more responsive, interactive and interesting, without the user having to wait for whole-page reloads. Ajax is seen as an important aspect of what is being called Web 2.0. Examples of Ajax techniques currently in use can be seen in Gmail, Google Maps etc.

Publishing Web Pages

Now the Web is available to individuals outside mass media. In order to "publish" a Web page, one does not have to go through a publisher or other media institution, and potential readers could be found in all corners of the globe. Unlike books and documents, hypertext does not need to have a linear order from beginning to end. It is not necessarily broken down into the hierarchy of chapters, sections, subsections, etc.

Many different kinds of information are now available on the Web, and for those who wish to know other societies, their cultures and peoples, it has become easier. When traveling in a foreign country or a remote town, one might be able to find some information about the place on the Web, especially if the place is in one of the developed countries. Local newspapers, government publications, and other materials are easier to access, and therefore the variety of information obtainable with the same effort may be said to have increased, for the users of the Internet.

Although some Web sites are available in multiple languages, many are in the local language only. Additionally, not all software supports all special characters, and RTL languages. These factors would challenge the notion that the World Wide Web will bring a unity to the world.

The increased opportunity to publish materials is certainly observable in the countless personal pages, as well as pages by families, small shops, etc., facilitated by the emergence of free Web hosting services.

According to a 2001 study, there were more than 550 million documents on the Web, mostly in the "invisible Web". A 2002 survey of 2,024 million Web pages determined that by far the most Web content was in English: 56.4%; next were pages in German (7.7%), French (5.6%) and Japanese (4.9%). A more recent study which used web searches in 75 different languages to sample the Web determined that there were over 11.5 billion web pages in the publicly indexable Web as of the end of January 2005.

Frustration over congestion issues in the Internet infrastructure and the high latency that results in slow browsing has led to an alternative name for the World Wide Web: the *World Wide Wait*. Speeding up the Internet is an ongoing discussion over the use of peering and QoS technologies. Other solutions to reduce the World Wide Wait can be found on W3C.

Standard guidelines for ideal Web response times are (Nielsen 1999, page 42):

1. 0.1 second (one tenth of a second). Ideal response time. The user doesn't sense any interruption.
2. 1 second. Highest acceptable response time. Download times above 1 second interrupt the user experience.
3. 10 seconds. Unacceptable response time. The user

experience is interrupted and the user is likely to leave the site or system.

These numbers are useful for planning server capacity.

Link Rot

The Web suffers from link rot, links becoming broken because of the continual disappearance or relocation of Web resources over time. The ephemeral nature of the Web has prompted many efforts to archive the Web. The Internet Archive is one of the most well-known efforts; they have been archiving the Web since 1996.

Ultimately, link rot is the price paid for the World Wide Web; the web's scale and infrastructure make it impossible to monitor all hyperlinks in real time, and there is no broadcast notification when a page is removed or renamed. Allowing links between independently maintained resources carries the inherent danger that some of the links will be invalidated over time.

Academic Conferences

The major academic event covering the WWW is the World Wide Web series of conferences, promoted by IW3C2. There is a list with links to all conferences in the series.

WWW Prefix in Web Addresses

"www" is commonly found at the beginning of Web addresses because of the long-standing practice of naming Internet hosts (servers) according to the services they provide. So for example, the host name for a Web server is often "www"; for an FTP server, "ftp"; and for a USENET news server, "news" or "nntp" (after the news protocol NNTP). These host names appear as DNS subdomain names, as in "www.example.com".

This use of such prefixes is not required by any technical standard; indeed, the first Web server was at "nxoc01.cern.ch" and even today many Web sites exist without a "www" prefix. The "www" prefix has no meaning in the way the main website is shown. The "www" prefix is simply one choice for a Web site's subdomain name.

Some Web browsers will automatically try adding "www." to the beginning, and possibly ".com" to the end, of typed URLs if no host is found without them. Internet Explorer, Mozilla Firefox and Opera will also prefix "http://www." and append ".com" to the address bar contents if the Control and Enter keys are pressed simultaneously. For example, entering "example" in the address bar and then pressing either just Enter or Control+Enter will usually resolve to "http://www.example.com", depending on the exact browser version and its settings.

Standards

The following is a cursory list of the documents that define the World Wide Web's three core standards:

1. Uniform Resource Locators (URL)
   - RFC 1738, Uniform Resource Locators (URL) (December 1994)
   - RFC 3986, Uniform Resource Identifier (URI): Generic Syntax (January 2005)
2. HyperText Transfer Protocol (HTTP)
   - RFC 1945, HTTP/1.0 specification (May 1996)
   - RFC 2616, HTTP/1.1 specification (June 1999)
   - RFC 2617, HTTP Authentication
   - HTTP/1.1 specification errata

3. Hypertext Markup Language (HTML)
   - Internet Draft, HTML version 1
   - RFC 1866, HTML version 2.0
   - HTML 3.2 Reference Specification
   - HTML 4.01 Specification
   - Extensible HTML (XHTML) Specification

Basically, the World Wide Web is the combination of four basic ideas:

(a) *Hypertext:* a format of information which allows, in a computer environment, one to move from one part of a document to another or from one document to another through internal connections among these documents (called "hyperlinks");

(b) *Resource Identifiers:* unique identifiers used to locate a particular resource (computer file, document or other resource) on the network—this is commonly known as a URL or URI, although the two have subtle technical differences;

(c) *The Client-server model of computing:* a system in which client software or a client computer makes requests of server software or a server computer that provides the client with resources or services, such as data or files; and

(d) *Markup language:* characters or codes embedded in text which indicate structure, semantic meaning, or advice on presentation.

On the World Wide Web, a client program called a user agent retrieves information resources, such as Web pages and other computer files, from Web servers using their URLs. If the user agent is a kind of Web browser, it displays the resources on a user's computer. The user can then follow hyperlinks in each web page to other World Wide Web resources, whose location is embedded in the hyperlinks. It is also possible, for example by filling in and submitting web forms, to post information back to a Web server for it to save or process in some way. Web pages are often arranged in collections of related material called "Web sites." The act of following hyperlinks from one Web site to another is referred to as *"browsing"* or sometimes as *"surfing"* the Web.

The phrase "surfing the Internet" was first made popular in print by Jean Armour Polly, a librarian, in an article called "Surfing the INTERNET", published in the University of Minnesota *Wilson Library Bulletin* in June 1992. Although Polly may have developed the phrase independently, slightly earlier uses of similar terms appeared on Usenet in 1991 and 1992, and some recollections claim it was also used verbally in the hacker community for a couple years before that.

For more information on the distinction between the World Wide Web and the Internet itself—as in everyday use the two are sometimes confused—see Dark internet where this is discussed in more detail. Although the English word *worldwide* is normally written as one word (without a space or hyphen), the proper name World Wide Web and abbreviation WWW are now well-established even in formal English. The earliest references to the Web called it the WorldWideWeb (an example of computer programmers' fondness for CamelCase) or the *World-Wide Web* (with a hyphen, this version of the name is the closest to normal English usage).

WEB BROWSERS AND INFORMATION TECHNOLOGY

Browsing is a term that refers to exploring an online area, usually on the World Wide Web. A web browser is a software application that enables a user to display and interact with text, images, and other information typically located on a web page at a website on the World Wide Web or a local area network. Text and images on a web page can contain hyperlinks to other web pages at the same or different website. Web browsers allow a user to quickly and easily access information provided on many web pages at many websites by traversing these links. Web browsers format HTML information for display, so the appearance of a web page may differ between browsers. Some of the web browsers available for personal computers include Internet Explorer, Mozilla Firefox, Safari, Opera, and Netscape in order of descending popularity (as of August 2006). Web browsers are the most commonly used type of HTTP user agent. Although browsers are typically used to access the World Wide Web, they can also be used to access information provided by web servers in private networks or content in file systems.

Standards and Protocols

Its communicate with web servers primarily using HTTP (hypertext transfer protocol) to fetch webpages. HTTP allows web browsers to submit information to web servers as well as fetch web pages from them. The most commonly used HTTP is HTTP/1.1, which is fully defined in RFC 2616. HTTP/1.1 has its own required standards that Internet Explorer does not fully support, but most other current-generation web browsers do. Pages are located by means of a URL (uniform resource locator, RFC 1738), which is treated as an address, beginning with *http:* for HTTP access. Many browsers also support a variety of other URL types and their corresponding protocols, such as *gopher:* for Gopher (a hierarchical hyperlinking protocol), *ftp:* for FTP (file transfer protocol), *rtsp:* for RTSP (real-time streaming protocol), and *https:* for HTTPS (an SSL encrypted version of HTTP). The file format for a web page is usually HTML (hyper-text markup language) and is identified in the HTTP protocol using a MIME *content type*. Most browsers natively support a variety of formats in addition to HTML, such as the JPEG, PNG and GIF image formats, and can be extended to support more through the use of plugins. The combination of HTTP *content type* and URL protocol specification allows web page designers to embed images, animations, video, sound, and streaming media into a web page, or to make them accessible through the web page.

Early web browsers supported only a very simple version of HTML. The rapid development of proprietary web browsers led to the development of non-standard dialects of HTML, leading to problems with Web interoperability. Modern web browsers support a combination of standards- and defacto-based HTML and XHTML, which should display in the same way across all browsers. No browser fully supports HTML 4.01, XHTML 1.x or CSS 2.1 yet. Currently many sites are designed using WYSIWYG HTML generation programs such as Macromedia Dreamweaver or Microsoft FrontPage. These often generate non-standard HTML by default, hindering the work of the W3C in developing standards, specifically with XHTML and CSS (cascading style sheets, used for page layout).

Some of the more popular browsers include additional components to support Usenet news, IRC (Internet relay chat), and e-mail. Protocols supported may include NNTP (network news transfer protocol), SMTP (simple mail transfer protocol), IMAP (Internet message access protocol), and POP (post office protocol). These browsers are often referred to as *Internet suites* or *application suites* rather than merely web.

A NeXTcube was used by Tim Berners-Lee (who pioneered the use of hypertext for sharing information) as the world's first web server, and also to write the first web browser, WorldWideWeb in 1990. Berners-Lee introduced it to colleagues at CERN in March 1991. Since then the development of web browsers has been inseparably intertwined with the development of the web itself.

Notably, the first browser, Silversmith, was created by John Bottoms in 1987. The browser, based on SGML tags, used a tag set from the Electronic Document Project of the AAP with minor modifications and was sold to a number of early adopters. At the time SGML was used exclusively for the formatting of printed documents. The use of SGML for electronically displayed documents signaled a shift in electronic publishing and was met with considerable resistance. Silversmith included an integrated indexer, full text searches, hypertext links between images text and sound using SGML tags and a return stack for use with hypertext links.

It included features that are still not available in today's browsers. These include capabilities such as the ability to restrict searches within document structures, searches on indexed documents using wild cards and the ability to search on tag attribute values and attribute names. In 1992, Tony Johnson releases the MidasWWW browser. Based on Motif/X, MidasWWW allows viewing of PostScript files on the Web from Unix and VMS, and even handles compressed PostScript. Another early popular web browser was ViolaWWW, which was modeled after HyperCard. However, the explosion in popularity of the web was triggered by NCSA Mosaic which was a graphical browser running originally on Unix but soon ported to the Apple Macintosh and Microsoft Windows platforms. Version 1.0 was released in September 1993, and was dubbed the killer application of the Internet. Marc Andreessen, who was the leader of the Mosaic team at NCSA, quit to form a company that would later be known as Netscape Communications Corporation. Netscape released its flagship Navigator product in October 1994, and it took off the next year.

Microsoft, which had thus far not marketed a browser (in fact even as late as 1995 Bill Gates dismissed personal use of the world wide web as a passing fad), finally entered the fray with its Internet Explorer product, purchased from Spyglass Inc. This began what is known as the *browser wars*, the fight for the web browser market between Microsoft and Netscape. The wars put the web in the hands of millions of ordinary PC users, but showed how commercialization of the web could stymie standards efforts. Both Microsoft and Netscape liberally incorporated proprietary extensions to HTML in their products, and tried to gain an edge by product differentiation, leading to the acceptance of the Microsoft proposed Cascading Style Sheets over Netscape's JavaScript Style Sheets (JSSS) by W3C.

In 1996, Netscape's share of the browser market reached 86% (with Internet Exporer edging up 10%); but then Microsoft began integrating its browser with its operating system and bundling deals with OEMs;, and within two years the trend had reversed. Although Microsoft have since faced antitrust litigation on these charges, the browser wars effectively ended once it was clear that Netscape's declining market share trend was irreversible.

Unable to continue commercially funding the product's development, Netscape responded by open sourcing its product, creating Mozilla. This did helped the browser maintain its technical edge over Internet Explorer, but did nothing to slow Netscape's declining market share. The company was purchased by America Online in late 1998. At first, the Mozilla project struggled to attract developers, but by 2002 it had evolved into a relatively stable and powerful internet suite. Mozilla 1.0 was released to mark this milestone.

Also in 2002, a spin off project that would eventually become the popular Mozilla Fiıefox was released. In 2004, Firefox 1.0 was released; Firefox 1.5 was released in November 2005. Firefox 2, a major update, was released in October 2006 and work has already begun on Firefox 3 which is scheduled for release in 2007. As of 2006, Mozilla and its derivatives account for approximately 12% of web traffic. Opera, an innovative, speedy browser popular in handheld devices, particularly mobile phones, as well as on PCs in some countries was released in 1996 and remains a niche player in the PC web browser market. It is available on Nintendo's DS, DS Lite and Wii consoles. The Opera Mini browser uses the Presto (layout engine) like all versions of Opera, but runs on most phones supporting Java Midlets.

It is remarkable, that Lynx browser remains popular for Unix shell users and with vision impaired users due to its entirely text-based nature. There are also several text-mode browsers with advanced features, such as w3m, Links (which can operate both in text and graphical mode), and the Links forks such as ELinks. The Macintosh scene too has traditionally been dominated by Internet Explorer and Netscape. However, Apple's Safari, the default browser on Mac OS X since version 10.3, has slowly grown to dominate this market. Browsers such as Firefox and Camino are also popular. In 2003, Microsoft announced that Internet Explorer would no longer be made available as a separate product but would be part of the evolution of its Windows platform, and that no more releases for the Macintosh would be made. However, in early 2005, Microsoft changed its plans, releasing version 7 of Internet Explorer for Windows XP, Windows Server 2003, and Windows Vista in October 2006.

Browsing Strategies

Browsing is a natural and effective approach to many types of information-seeking problems. It is natural because it coordinates human physical, emotive, and cognitive resources in the same way that humans monitor the physical world and search for physical objects. It can be effective because the environment and particularly human-created environments are generally organised and highly redundant - especially information environments that are designed according to organisational principles.

Browsing is particularly effective for information problems that are ill defined or interdisciplinary and when the goal of information seeking is to gather overview information about a topic or to keep abreast of developments in a field. The term *browsing* is used in a variety of settings, including forestry, zoology, architectural design, marketing, and information science (Chang and Rice, 1993). The computer and information science literature uses the term *browsing* simply to mean navigating, scanning, and scrolling, and many interfaces include "browsers" that allow users to move across or within screens, windows, records, and databases.

Generally, in traditional library literature, browsing was most often associated with card catalogs or bookshelves. More recently, Bates (1989) argued for the importance of browsing in conjunction with other online search strategies. We term this *across-document browsing,* because the information seeker browses through records or books to find items to examine more closely. The education and reading literature also have been concerned with perusing a document to extract its gist or to locate a relevant passage, with the terms *skimming, scanning* and *browsing* used to distinguish this activity from reading or studying. We term this type of browsing *within-document browsing* and believe it to be a high-priority research problem for electronic environments.

Most types of across-document browsing identify specific documents or objects that may then be browsed or studied according to the information seekers's needs. One exception is across-document browsing in a collection to gain a sense of scope or form. Thus, browsing is a term whose meaning must be taken from its context. A significant characteristic of browsing in electronic environments is the blurring of boundaries between document collections or databases and discrete documents or records. The implication for design is to provide systems that support seamless browsing across and within documents. A hypertext collection of articles may be considered a single document when linked to other hypertexts or as a collection of documents (nodes) in its own right. In either case, a single node or a collection of nodes is represented on the same display device, and the display is controlled by the same paging, scrolling, and windowing actions. In the current electronic environments, there are no clear delineations for the user in either the physical display device or the physical actions taken to execute browsing activity. This situation is exacerbated in networked environments in which documents from different databases appear in the same window or the same document is represented in different databases.

In regard to the information-seeking framework browsing strategies are more dependent than analytical strategies are on interactions between the information seeker and the system. The system also has more influence on the progress of the search during browsing.

Also, during browsing, the information-seeking subprocesses proceed in somewhat more parallel fashion; more time is spent in the examination subprocess; and there are a wider variety of cycles in the overall process.

Browsing offers significant challenges to information seekers and system designers.

First, an entry point must be identified. Determining an entry point combines problem definition and query formulation. Entry points can be determined by random selection, by the use of indexes or statistical analyses that return a set of items for browsing, and by opportunistic, iterative examination. The challenge to the information seeker is to relate personal knowledge about the topic to what the system represents and how its representations are organised. The challenge to designers is to make clear the system's scope and organisation and to suggest entry points to the searcher.

Second, information must be examined and assessed during browsing. The information seeker's challenge is to make rapid judgments of relevance, and the designer's challenge is to provide flexible display facilities for examination and assessment. These challenges illustrate how browsing blurs the information-seeking subprocesses. Problem definition, query formulation, execution, examination, and iteration are especially intertwined during browsing. This fluidity and integration is caused by the parallel engagement of physical, perceptual, and cognitive processes during browsing; to the close coupling between the information seeker and the organisations and representations provided by the information environment; and to the open-ended information problems that lend themselves to browsing. This chapter is based on the notion that the natural human inclination to browse and the organisations inherent in information systems are strongly reinforced and harmonised in highly interactive electronic environments that complement and invite browsing. Based on this perspective, we argue for a design philosophy that amplifies human abilities and inclinations rather than one that optimises organisation and task analysis. We consider the variety of reasons that people browse, different types of browsing behavior, limitations of browsing, and the ways that manual and electronic information systems can support browsing.

Applications

Browsing is used for many purposes and is manifested in different ways. In contrast with analytical strategies, in which goal definition is important to success and efficiency, browsing strategies may be applied to more informal or general goals and depend more heavily on the information encountered during the search. We browse to gain an overview of a physical or conceptual space. By scanning a scene or a document, we can identify key landmarks and characteristics and use them to form impressions of the scene or document and to make analogies to known scenes or concepts.

For example, by scanning the title page, table of contents, section headings, index, and reference list of a book, we gain a sense of the content's scope, depth of coverage, and the author's organisational perspective and thereby can decide quickly whether to invest time reading it. It is important to note that in the case of books, those attributes that we browse first are well-established standards to aid browsing. Hildreth (1982) pointed out that these features of books both encourage and enhance browsing. Electronic environments are only beginning to build in systematic support for browsing. We can browse software applications by spending a few minutes traversing menus, executing generic commands or manipulating system objects, and examining the form and scope of help and instructions. At this point in the development of the science of interface design, it is unclear how a program or a database should "reveal itself" to users to encourage and enhance browsing.

Full-text CD-ROM databases allow users to browse through texts by jumping to highlighted query terms, but these systems are limited by the display technology. Browsing Internet news groups or World Wide Web nodes gives a sense of breadth to various groups and details of specific postings but few organisational cues to the scope and organisation of all the groups. Another reason that we browse is to monitor a process. When driving, we regularly check how close we are to the road shoulder, look for landmarks and signs, and glance in the rear view mirror to check the status of cars near to us. When systematically examining books on a shelf, we often jump ahead to gain a sense of how much time we will need to complete our browsing.

Some electronic search systems provide history or path tools so that users can quickly go back and examine the progress of their search. Readers often scan forward in a book or article to see what remains and to establish an anticipatory frame of reference or scan backward to review what has been read and regain or revise their sense of context. These actions are indicative of the text reinspection-reading strategy used by skilled readers in comprehending text (Garner, 1987).

This type of browsing is particularly important for ongoing, accretional information seeking in which the objective is to stay abreast of a field. Many information environments provide aids for monitoring such as sidebars, pull quotes, abstracts, review articles, and book reviews. Developing interfaces that support and amplify browsing through the mass of information created in a domain is a critical problem in information science and human-computer interaction. We also browse because it requires a smaller cognitive load than analytical search strategies do. Browsing is highly dependent on human perceptual abilities to recognise relevant information. Analytical query formulations require us to apply cognitive resources to recall from memory specific terms that represent the concepts related to our problem. Taken to an extreme, the advantage of a smaller cognitive load may be abused.

For example, because of cognitive laziness, information seekers may apply minimal cognitive effort and simply depend on perceptual and motor processes to stumble on relevant information. In general, however, applying recognition allows the information seeker to concentrate more cognitive resources on the problem at hand. For tasks that are ill defined or complex, browsing allows information seekers to devote full cognitive resources to problem definition and system manipulation and to involve the perceptual system in filtering words or images. Besides bringing additional resources from the perceptual system, there may be symbiotic advantages to applying multiple subsystems that are mutually reinforcing - in effect, the whole result is greater than the sum of its parts. This parallelism effect is perhaps even stronger because browsing requires high levels of direct physical engagement by the information seeker; that is, we must move, scan, scroll, jump, and page more quickly through the shelves, pages, or screens. Thus, browsing may be more of a direct manipulation strategy than the formal methods are because it involves cognitive, perceptual, and motor systems concurrently and continually.

Using both physical and mental subsystems in coordinated activity may reinforce experience and memory for events. Our interviews with and observations of students using the Perseus system suggest that there may be some positive interactions between the physical actions of using a lexicon and the cognitive actions of translating Greek into English. The popularity of video games and simulations that use high degrees of direct manipulation also illustrates the importance of engaging multiple subsystems in complex activity. Our understanding of how the satisfaction associated with direct manipulation affects performance and learning is very poor. There is no definitive evidence whether learners remember more as a result of coordinating their physical and mental subsystems or how intellectual task performance such as information seeking is affected.

If performance can be improved by engaging physical and mental subsystems more closely, there must be design efforts to coordinate physical and intellectual actions at workstations. Furthermore, for some specific types of information seeking, such as locating intermediate facts in a chain of processes or repetitive lookups, experience and memory should be minimised and speed and accuracy maximised.

While seeking information, we also browse to clarify

the information problem. Because many of our problems are due to anomalous states of knowledge, browsing a space of information in the problem domain can help us clarify and expand our knowledge. We may retrieve a record, article, or book and examine it quickly to look for ideas about entry terms, alternative or related concepts or to learn more about the problem so that we can clarify it and state it in precise language. Likewise, we browse to find something interesting that suggests a more specific or exciting problem that we can then attack more formally. For example, in our study of attorneys and law intermediaries, the subjects noted that one reason to go online rather than use inexpensive printed sources was that the problem was ill defined (Marchionini *et al.,* 1993). The electronic systems allowed these information seekers to quickly locate sets of legal documents that provided feedback to clarify what issues were involved in the problem. Related to problem clarification, people browse to stimulate or develop a plan or a formal strategy. An information seeker may use a simple query to retrieve a large number of generally related documents and browse through the title words or subject headings to determine technical vocabulary, identify related facets, and generally get to know the intellectual neighborhood before formulating a specific set of formal queries. This strategy is particularly useful if the information seeker is not an expert in the domain or when controlled vocabulary lists or thesauri are unavailable. We also browse to discover and learn. Regardless of how comprehensive our efforts are to investigate an area, we all experience the pleasure of serendipitous discoveries that are highly relevant to our information problems but found in surprising places and situations. Browsing is an activity that may yield new insights in two ways. On one hand, we may locate a highly relevant item by browsing through resources beyond those systematically coded and assigned as relevant. This has a low probability but a high payoff- like an intellectual lottery. This is the basis of many arguments for serendipity. For example, we may find a highly relevant paper that was not indexed with the terms guiding the search, or we may locate an alternative special-interest group.

On the other hand, we may not locate any specific document that would otherwise have been missed but, rather, gain new insights or interesting associations for our problem by browsing through alternative sources that use different tools, techniques, and data structures. Scholars are highly conscious of such possibilities and support institutional policies to facilitate such serendipity, for example, open stacks in libraries and cross-disciplinary colloquia.

Notably, by browsing in an unfamiliar field, we may discover methodologies that have not been applied to our own field or gain new perspectives or metaphors to apply to our own work. In interdisciplinary fields like information science, scholars must use results from the many allied fields. In many cases they work at the boundaries of several fields and depend on browsing to span the boundaries to gain synthetic insights and integrate concepts. For example, Auster and Choo (1993) have noted that executives depend on scanning information sources across traditional boundaries to stay abreast of their field.

Finally, we browse because the environment invites browsing - in fact, stores and museums are carefully designed to stimulate browsing. The organisations in nature and created by civilisation invite interaction and exploration. The importance of how systems invite and support browsing is considered in a subsequent section. Browsing has become much more important as more information resources migrate to electronic environments. The interactivity characteristic of these environments affects all the reasons for browsing above but has particularly interesting possibilities for discovery and learning. Humans decide how to use their time and resources for this type of information seeking according to constraints on these resources, probabilities for finding new knowledge, and payoffs for new knowledge.

For example, during a brainstorming phase of information seeking or at an impasse in the process, if 20 minutes are available to invest in an environment (e.g., a library), a min-max heuristic may be applied to examine low-probability sources to gain high-payoff information that may suggest directions for beginning or restarting work. Electronic environments provide a good place to lessen time constraints and raise the probabilities of locating high-payoff information. First, electronic environments are more accessible and may invite more frequent explorations. Second, electronic environments can improve the likelihood of a payoff, by providing feedback that the user can control directly or a profile can control automatically.

Browsing Limitations

Basically, Browsing requires the information seeker to perceive all potentially pertinent information items, and each perception requires time. This "on-the-fly" processing has several consequences. Humans fatigue quickly, especially when doing repetitive tasks. Most studies of information-seeking behavior use subjects in a laboratory setting, in which performance motivation is influenced by study conditions. The Wiberley and Daugherty (1988) work discussed earlier suggests an upper limit of 200 items as the number of citations that users are willing to scan in electronic environments, although these results were based on surveys of the literature and systems designed to discourage examination of long lists of citations. Lee and Whalen (1993) studied an automated "mug shot" system for helping crime witnesses identify suspects. They reviewed consistent results from multiple sources indicating that performance accuracy falls off rapidly between 100 and 200 image examinations. There is no evidence for how persistent users are when browsing through electronic texts and what factors influence persistence and fatigue. In fact, there is a need to determine a variety of physiological-psychological limits for browsing in various environments. Browsing offers severe temporal penalties when the search task is well defined and a structured search system is available.

If indexes or electronic search tools are available and the information problem can be represented in terms of the indexing language or parameters of the tool, then a formal query is likely to be more efficient. Furthermore, if the information space is ordered and a known unit is to be located, application of even a simple binary, search strategy will be more efficient than scanning the list in order. The value of the information seeker's time and any time-sensitive charges may also discourage browsing. In addition to the efficiency limitations of browsing in large information spaces, browsing may also limit the coverage that is possible.

Thus, inefficiencies may lead to less effectiveness. It is mainly for these reasons that professional intermediaries are trained to avoid browsing in order to save connect charges and personal time. Users who are browsing primary materials have not only these monetary concerns but also the problem of not being distracted by "interesting details" of the context. The nature of opportunistic browsing strategies in particular may decrease the effectiveness of browsing and lead to disorientation or distraction, especially in systems that offer few navigational cues. Observational strategies are particularly prone to distraction, and navigation tactics can lead to both disorientation and distraction. Garner, Gillingham, and White (1989) described how children and highly skilled adult readers are subject to "seductive details" while reading nonfiction passages. Their work showed that interesting details about the topic of interest distracted both types of reader from recognising and recalling the main points of the text. Browsing situations and highly interactive environments must certainly exacerbate this effect.

As people browse, they may make discoveries, but they also may be distracted, confused, disoriented, or frustrated by peripheral and tangential information. This is especially problematic when browsing is driven by the need for an overview of an area or to get a sense of a text. In relation to distraction, which wastes time and may mislead information seekers, browsing in rich environments may also lead to information overload. This is especially true in highly interconnected electronic environments in which the richness of relationships leads to confusion and overload rather than a deeper understanding of the concepts represented by the system.

Clearly, tools and strategies for minimi/ing distraction and overload are needed. In addition to affecting efficiency and effectiveness directly, browsing strategies may have subtle influences on information-seeking performance. Browsing strategies are attention dependent, relying heavily on recognition, and human attention is biased toward what we know and like. Therefore, what we recognise and attend to naturally is biased. Our observations of users of various search systems illustrate the human tendency toward "wishful thinking" as information seekers patch together bits of evidence rooted in availability rather than logical similarity.

An artifact of electronic systems is what may be termed *cognitive laziness,* a malady invited by systems that allow mindless search or browsing. Users flounder under the illusion of productivity as they enter queries or scan items without reflection or inference. A related bias may be termed *cognitive inertia,* a tendency to continue following paths or lines of evidence rather than examining contrary or alternative directions. Linear text reinforces such thinking, and this may be one of the best information transfer qualities from author to reader.

However, nonlinear environments offered by electronics discourage such information flow and may lead to breakdowns in information transfer. Because technology usually has not been specifically designed to support browsing, there are hardware and software limitations on electronic browsing. The requirement of using a display device has so far limited how users can take advantage of the designers' physical and spatial creativity in regard to retrieval. Intellectual space must be broken across screens or windows that are temporal rather than static - all the pages of a book may look alike, but each page is a distinct physical entity. Because all the information objects used on a display are confined by the same static area and position, users are unable to use physical characteristics such as size, shape, thickness, or paper quality as access points for locating those objects.

Because there is good evidence that human memory is episodic (e.g., Walker and Kintsch, 1985), the absence of physical cues to distinguish different intellectual experiences makes people even more dependent on symbolic retrieval mechanisms that cannot be manipulated directly. Browsing strategies, like many other problem-solving methods, are subject to a law of diminishing returns. The limitations of browsing parallel the limits of full-text searching. Although there is evidence that adding additional terms to a query statement will improve recall in full-text systems (Gomez, Lochbaum, and Land-auer, 1990), such improvements must have limits because the salience of the additional words must eventually decrease as various facets of the concept are exhausted; that is, eventually, all documents will be retrieved. Likewise, total reliance on browsing will yield a superficial perspective on a limited portion of an information space.

Analytical search, browsing, and careful reading or study all have roles to play in most information-seeking problems. The key to using browsing strategies is selectively using them for appropriate problems and with those search systems that best support it. Users who simply wish to retrieve information in primary systems rather than learn about the context of the information may choose to use intermediaries to minimise costs or avoid the limits of the strategy.

Support for browsing across objects is built into many environments. Streets and buildings are organised to direct physical movement, and museums and stores invite users to explore personal interests while providing overall organisational constraints. As Zoellick (1987) stated, "Browsing presumes a document collection is structured in some way." Although browsing can be used (and perhaps is the only approach to use) in random collections, organised environments make most browsing strategies much easier. Product catalogs group together like items for easy perusal and comparison and place related groups nearby to suggest other products that customers may purchase.

Video controllers and automobile radios provide scanning mechanisms to quickly browse through their respective information spectra. Libraries that provide open stacks to patrons shelve books according to a classification system that groups related books together, thus mapping conceptual similarities onto physical proximity on the shelves. A major limitation of this arrangement is that each book can exist in only one shelf location but may be related to many topics.

Electronic libraries can overcome this limitation because the electronic document can be instantiated at many places in the classification system; that is, electronic systems are able to manage many-to-many relationships. Although this potential has yet to be tapped, the probability of locating a specific item by browsing through an electronic catalog that assigns items to many main topics is likely to be greater than the probability of locating the specific item by browsing through only physical shelves. Objects such as books also provide structural support for browsing. Tables of contents, chapter and section headings, and indexes are provided to make the organisation of a book explicit and to allow users to examine contents in a nonlinear fashion. Journal articles offer abstracts and organisational structures such as headings and tables that support browsing and nonlinear reading.

Some journals require specific organisational structures and promote browsing in various ways. Medical journals often provide augmentations such as sidebars, use typographic techniques like placing methodology sections in type font sizes that are smaller than those of other sections, and require authors to write structured abstracts (Huth, 1987).

Electronic documents can provide the same types of support for browsing and offer additional elements such as hypertextual links that invite browsing. Most browsing is highly interactive and blurs distinctions among the information-seeking subprocesses. Determining an entry point combines search system selection and query formulation; examination, extraction, iteration, and problem definition progress concurrently as the browsing continues. A primary challenge for electronic systems is to support this close coupling of the information-seeking subprocesses. Closely linking input and output mechanisms is one way to parallel and reinforce highly dynamic browsing behavior. Users initiate queries or probes in the database, and the system displays results that the user in turn rapidly manipulates. Thus, input mechanisms for query formulation and display control must be provided by the system seamlessly and rapidly so that user control and system display are synchronised.

Various types of electronic information systems support browsing (e.g., bibliographic, full-text, hypertext, image databases, hypermedia), and different techniques have been demonstrated (e.g., text processing, image processing, visual browsers, and information retrieval techniques) that support browsing. However, today's systems provide only one or two features or techniques added on to support browsing as a secondary strategy to analytical search (e.g., allowing users to page or scroll through document sets of title's returned by a query). Electronic environments offer significant possibilities to support browsing as well as analytical search strategies. In fact, electronic systems that support combinations of browsing and analytical strategies are the most helpful to users choosing the most appropriate strategy for the problem. Many systems claim to support browsing, thereby demonstrating the widespread recognition of the need for such systems and for specific techniques and mechanisms. There is a dearth of evidence, however, related to how browsing in these environments affects information-seeking performance, which techniques and mechanisms are most applicable to different search tasks and with what user populations, and how these techniques and mechanisms may best be combined and integrated into general-purpose search systems. Examples of systems that illustrate one or more of these techniques and features follow.

The examples are organised by generic type of database represented (bibliographic, full text, and graphical) and by types of mechanisms (visual queries and browsers, information retrieval techniques). These examples are not meant to be exhaustive but just to show some of the ways that browsing is supported in current systems. Early OPAC systems did very little to support subject searching at all, let alone support browsing (Hildreth, 1982). Second-generation OPACs provided for subject access by allowing queries to be posed according to controlled subject headings (e.g., Library of Congress Subject Headings) and, in many cases, through keywords in the title. Several of these systems refer to one of these access methods as browsing, leading to more confusion about what browsing means. Beheshti (1992) noted that current OPACs lack display characteristics to allow browsing and proposed a graphic interface that represents MARC records visually rather than simply textually. Other OPACs have also used graphic interfaces to aid users in browsing through either the bibliographic records or the book surrogates (e.g.. The Science Library Catalog of Borgman et al., 1990; Pejtersen's 1989 Book House system) and provide alternative strategies for search, including hypertext-like browsing capabilities. Studies of children showed that they used picture browsing (various icons) almost as much as they did analytical search strategies and that they were highly satisfied with the interface and their results. OPAC designers have begun to consider browsing as a legitimate search strategy, but this is not generally the case for online systems because connect charges encourage off-line planning and analytical strategies.

Because bibliographic databases on CD-ROM are not constrained by connect charges, some systems provide browsing support in the form of highlighted query terms, scrollable indexes, and jumps between query terms in text. Allen (1992) found that perceptual speed and cognitive abilities such as logical reasoning and verbal comprehension influenced information seeking in a CD-ROM bibliographic database. This free-text searching was named *browse* and it was the option most often selected.

Based on these results, Allen recommended that the display of linear lists of hits be modified for users who lack perceptual speed, perhaps using a hierarchical display of document lists. His results are related to those of Vicente, Hayes, and Williges (1987) who reported the importance of spatial ability to users of hierarchical file systems. These results are interesting because they remind designers to consider browsers' perceptual and spatial abilities.

Given the quantity of text that professionals must deal with, techniques for browsing through full-text systems are important. Tenopir (1985) noted that full-text searching allows users to make immediate judgments about relevance and recommended that careful consideration be given to how text is displayed. She also found that documents containing more than 10 occurrences of a query word or the word occurring in four or more paragraphs had an average precision three times higher than the overall precision. These results demonstrate that statistical analyses of terms and documents should be useful in helping information seekers select entry points for within-document browsing and in locating promising sets of documents when browsing across documents.

Tenopir and Ro (1990) noted that users frequently browsed through articles for background information on topics and required good scrolling capabilities as well as multiple windows to allow several documents to be used at the same time. Three techniques have provided clear advantages for browsing: string-search capability, highlighted terms in the text, and hypertext links. First, string search is available in most hypertext and other full-text search systems, serving as the principal way to query and probe the database for promising entry points. Liebscher's 1992 work demonstrated users' preferences for string search even over hypertext links. Second, highlighting query terms in a text is a simple but effective way of supporting browsing and information seeking in general. Much of our work at the University of Maryland showed that users make good use of highlighted query terms in electronic encyclopedias, computer science articles, and legal literature.

Many users jumped from highlighted term to highlighted term rather than paging or scrolling. Egan and colleagues (1989) also found that highlighting query terms was a powerful tool for subjects using a SuperBook version of a statistics book. Third, the essence of hypertext is browsing by following links, and the development of hypertext systems has led to an interest in browsing techniques from both physical and conceptual interface perspectives. Hypertext systems support both explicit links among text fragments by means of highlighted terms or phrases (embedded menus; Shneiderman, 1992) and implicit links by means of string search or pull-down menus.

Other developments have improved the browsability of electronic text. Larger screens, better type font and size control, and better screen layouts have somewhat reduced the penalties of reading text on a screen rather than on paper (e.g., Hansen and Haas, 1989), although reading text on electronic displays takes longer than reading paper documents does (Gould et al., 1987). Many full-text systems provide simple ways to scroll, page, jump to the next highlighted term, and jump to the next document in a list, and skilled users may be able to use such features to mitigate reading-speed penalties. More important, these mechanisms for moving rapidly within texts should facilitate browsing and it remains to be determined how browsing speeds differ in paper and electronic settings. A variety of techniques to structure and display hypertext links have been proposed and tested. Furuta and Stotts (Furuta and Stotts, 1989; Stotts and Furuta, 1989) defined a browsing semantics based on a Petri net model to limit how users navigate hyperdocuments. Their Trellis system can determine whether or not a link should be active, depending on previous traversal events. It helps users make browsing decisions by displaying the current state of the network and four text windows related to nodes in the net.

Search Systems for Graphics

Improved computing systems have led to the development of image databases. Slide collections, clip art, images of magazines or journals, and video sequences have been made accessible in a variety of ways. Most image collections can be searched only through words or phrases assigned to each image. Some systems provide close linkages between words found in texts and images.

For example, the city Olynthus described in a textual passage in Perseus can be used to bring up a site plan and an image of a coin minted there. These linkages can be found through a word search that locates all occurrences in texts as well as occurrences in catalog cards that use the target word somewhere in the description of the object (all objects are attached to catalog cards, which may contain multi-paragraph textual descriptions in addition to basic identification and provenance information). Although these systems provide good access to either analog or digital images, browsing is often tedious, owing to the time it takes to retrieve and display images.

These approaches also depend on access through textual descriptions rather than graphic properties. A technique that directly supports browsing through images should provide what are called *thumbnails* or miniatures (Nielsen, 1990b) of the images. Erickson and Salomon (1991) described an interface to a large-scale news story database that includes browsing support through what they term "bird's eye views" of the database. These views are miniature displays of articles that show surrounding articles and graphics. Information seekers can scroll through these views and use visual cues to select and display the text or images in a large window.

The Perseus Project has a thumbnail browser that displays up to nine miniature views of graphics objects in the corpus. Users can rapidly scan through these miniatures before selecting and displaying detailed views to study. Another approach to supporting graphical search is to let users pose a graphical query. A system developed by Garber and Grunes (1992) permits art directors to search an image database by either providing an example image to act as a template or selecting criteria from menus.

This interface was designed according to a careful study of how art directors actually search for images and demonstrates how important this task analysis and these customised interfaces are to different problem areas. This approach is an analog of word queries, and progress in pattern-matching research may make such systems more viable. A combined graphic and textual approach to chromosome mapping is the Image-Query interface at the Lawrence Berkeley Laboratory (U.S. Department of Energy, 1992). As part of the Chromosome Information System, this interface allows researchers to specify queries or browse through miniature icons of the images. Buttons for zooming in to different magnifications of the image and displaying textual descriptions and parameters are provided in a multiple-window environment. A different approach to accessing image collections is to compress image collections by displaying only the most significant elements or scenes. This is particularly useful for film or video.

Rorvig (1993) described a method for "abstracting" video, that is, for selecting frames from video sequences that results in 700:1 compression for scanning visual documents. Frames are selected according to a set of visual characteristics (e.g., hue, line frequency, angle frequency) and a statistical analysis that focuses on large deviations in characteristics. Elliot and Davenport (1994) have developed a technique that displays each frame of video as a line in a composite image (block) that represents about 30 seconds of play.

Thus a single glance can easily identify scene changes. The block can be viewed in real time as the video plays, which allows viewers to monitor specific patterns. Although users must become familiar with decoding the graphical patterns, this system illustrates another way to compress video by using only specific components of each video frame. These examples demonstrate that the current state of work on browsing graphics databases is concentrating on finding workable representations and mechanisms, that is, technical developments. As more technical alternatives are developed, they will advance our understanding of how users work in graphics databases and what principles should guide interface design. Such progress is crucial as video and other moving images are included in digital libraries and video-on-demand services.

Visual Queries and Browsers

Since representing information graphically has long been recognised as a powerful way to aid understanding and dissemination (Tufte, 1990; Tukey, 1977), and there is substantial interface work under way to develop visualisation tools for scientific phenomena. Graphical approaches to information retrieval have also been proposed and developed, especially for database management systems (e.g., Fogg, 1984; Herot, 1980). Larson (1986) described a visual approach to browsing through well-structured databases. His system supports four types of browsing operations: structuring objects for examination, filtering objects, panning to nearby objects, and zooming in to different levels of detail. Users perform these operations by manipulating a graphical scheme that shows database objects and relationships.

Travers (1989) developed a hypertext interface for the CYC database that uses boxes to represent hierarchical relationships among nodes. Color saturation is also used to reinforce semantic distances among outer and embedded boxes. A technique proposed by Purnas (1986) gives users ways to focus on objects of interest while maintaining a sense of context through peripheral views of the database. An intuitively appealing approach to viewing an information space, his "fisheye" views have been implemented in several systems, including SuperBook (Egan et al., 1989). Perhaps the most extensive collection of graphical techniques was that implemented by Card, Mackinlay, and Robertson at Xerox. Based on a general cognitive model of human performance and using three-dimensional graphical techniques, their systems allow users to view and manipulate significantly more information per screen than other interfaces do. Their perspective wall displays three sides of a rectangular solid in perspective so that the "front" wall shows a large rectangular array of cells and the two "side" walls angle back in perspective with diminishing arrays of cells (Mackinlay, Robertson, and Card, 1991).

Users can easily slide walls to bring arrays of interest into front view. Another technique uses "cone trees" to represent large hierarchical structures that users can rotate and manipulate to find information (Robertson, Mackinlay, and Card, 1991). In one example, 600 directories comprising 10,000 files were represented on a single display. These techniques offer promising directions for systems that support browsing through high-performance displays, although they require sophisticated workstations. Another collaborative effort that involved many researchers is the work of Shneiderman and his colleagues at the University of Maryland Human- Computer Interaction Laboratory. This work applies direct manipulation techniques to information seeking under the name of *dynamic queries.* Systems that support dynamic-queries provide sliders for setting interval data values and hierarchical menus to select categorical data values and immediately display the results of settings. A museum system allowed users to select types of archaeological sites, historical periods, dates of visit, and participation costs (Plaisant, 1993).

Another implementation permits users to manipulate sliders for cost, location, number of bedrooms, and other house features, to visualise what homes were on the market (Williamson and Shneiderman, 1992). Each change of slider immediately resulted in an updated map with the available homes plotted on it. This approach is intuitive and pleasing to use, and the users in their study consistently conducted faster searches with this system than with paper or natural language interfaces. This type of system may be best for problems that lend themselves to graphical representation and have ordinal criterion values. Another representation called *tree maps* uses horizontal and vertical slices and color to display large hierarchical structures such as directories of files (Shneiderman, 1990).

Using this technique, directories of over 1000 files can be browsed through according to various parameters such as size and file type. Although traditional information retrieval research is aimed at optimising analytical search, often omitting informal browsing strategics, many of the fruits of information retrieval work may be applied to systems that invite and support browsing across documents. The most obvious information retrieval advance to support browsing is relevance feedback. The relevance feedback adjusts users' queries based on assessments of retrieved documents. In a review of relevance feedback, Harmon (1992) reported that variations of relevance feedback doubled the performance of the systems she tested. The best techniques were those that expanded queries rather than simply reweighting terms in the original query. She found that expanding with only 20 selected terms was superior to expanding with all terms. This seems to be another example of a law of diminishing returns in specifying terms in queries - more terms are generally better but after a point, too many terms either lead to intolerably low precision or do not yield any additional recall.

Systems with relevance feedback interfaces include Salton's SMART system (Salton and McGill, 1983), Frisse's *Dynamic Medical Handbook* (Frisse and Cousins, 1989),

Williams's RABBIT system (Williams, 1984), Walker's OK API (Walker, 1987), and Erickson and Salomon's *Desktop Information System* (Erickson and Salomon, 1991).

The Wide Area Information Server (WAIS) interface has become popular for searching Internet sources and uses relevance feedback (Kahle and Medlar, 1991). Relevance feedback is like browsing in that it depends on feedback as the user explores and probes the system interactively. The underlying mechanisms of relevance feedback depend on statistical or probabilistic techniques, but these may be hidden from the end users. However, future systems could permit sophisticated browsers to manipulate the underlying relevance feedback parameters (e.g., how terms are reweighted for query modification, what terms are used for query expansion).

Another collection of information retrieval techniques connected with browsing interfaces are clustering algorithms. Salton (1989) noted that browsing is promoted by the proximity of similar documents that results from clustering. Cutting, Karger, Pedersen, and Tukey (1992) reported a technique that applies clustering to allow browsing of large databases. Their "scatter and gather" technique is specifically designed to assist users in exploring open-ended or,ill-defined problems and to work in conjunction with analytical approaches as needed. They contrast searching an index in a book that requires a term or query with examining a table of contents that offers a sense of what types of questions the book may answer, and they base the browsing part of their scatter and gather approach on the latter.

The basic approach is to use a clustering algorithm to scatter the collection into document clusters and to report the cluster summaries to the user. Based on which clusters the user chooses for further study, the system gathers these clusters and reclusters them to produce a smaller scattering. The process continues until there is a small number of documents that can be examined individually. The increasing computational power of computers has prompted some researchers to combine sophisticated information retrieval techniques with graphics display techniques to support browsing. Korfhage (1991) created a technique for reducing the high dimensionality of a document space to display graphically the space according to the users' queries and profiles. The queries and profiles are reference points from which all other documents are distanced according to similarity metrics.

High-resolution display of the distance space allows users to view clusters of documents according to their own queries and profiles rather than some absolute clustering based on frequencies and co-occurrences alone. Korfhage's GU1DO system illustrates a pioneering approach to personalised graphical views of Semistructured document collections. Lin (1993) proposed a framework for presenting two-dimensional displays of document collections that is based on a neural network clustering of documents. He used Kohonen's feature map algorithm to cluster documents and prepare a graphical map that represents topic importance by area size and topic similarity by proximity. Instead of ranking documents in linear fashion based on some similarity measure, the algorithm maps the collection's high-dimensional vector representation of titles to a two-dimensional map that preserves similarity through geometric distance.

The resulting map defines areas for topical clusters that are juxtaposed with semantically similar clusters and whose areas are proportional to the frequency of occurrence in the corpus. Lin compared his computer-generated maps with maps produced by humans and found that the subjects could use the different maps equally effectively to locate titles. Both the computer-generated maps and those produced by humans werse superior to a random map. Although generating such maps is computationally expensive at this time, such maps offer good possibilities for supporting the informal information-seeking strategies collated under the term *browsing.*

Four different browsing strategies were defined according to how the various information-seeking factors interact during information seeking. Limitations of browsing were discussed, and the importance of the environment was illustrated with examples of systems that support various aspects of browsing. Clearly, browsing strategies and analytical strategies complement each other, and systems should support the preferences and abilities of diverse users.

Reviews of browsing (Chang and Rice, 1993; Hildreth, 1982) cite a number of typologies developed by different investigators. Although there are differences in how the types are named, there seems to be agreement on three general types of browsing that may be differentiated by the object of search (the information needed) and by the systematicity of tactics used. At one extreme, users perform directed (Herner, 1970) or specific (Apted, 1971) browsing. This form of browsing is systematic and focused and is often driven by a specific object or target. For example, scanning a list for a known item is a highly directed type of browsing because the objective is specific and known by the information seeker. Tasks such as verifying information or retrieving dates or other facts require repetitive and systematic browsing behavior. A second type of browsing is semidirected and predictive (Herner, 1970) or generally purposeful (Apted, 1971).

This type of browsing has a less definite target and proceeds less systematically, for example, entering a single, general term into a full-text electronic database and casually examining the retrieved records. This type of browsing allows various degrees of target definition but requires multiple probes of the system and thus is time-consuming. A third type of browsing is undirected (Herner, 1970) or general (Apted, 1971) browsing that is characterised as having no real goal and very little focus - more like recreation than information seeking; for example, repeatedly changing television channels to find something of interest to watch. In addressing browsing in electronic systems, Cove and Walsh (1988) and others described a similar trio of browsing types based on the not-quite orthogonal dimensions of goal definition and behavioral systematicity. Thus, types of browsing have been characterised coarsely according to the specificity of the object sought, which in turn influences the systematicity of actions the information seeker takes while browsing. These three different degrees of systematicity are from most to least systematic, *systematic, opportunistic,* and *casual* browsing. Systematic browsing exemplifies more linear sequencing and regular iterations of the information-seeking subprocesses; opportunistic browsing jumps Mm examination to many different subprocesses; and casual browsing exemplifies almost random sequences of information-seeking subprocesses. Such behavioral characterisations are useful for describing browsing as an information-seeking strategy, but a more detailed and cognitively oriented analysis is required to understand browsing, especially in regard to the role of the object of information sought. One step in this direction is Kwasnik's study (1992) of how people browsed through paper, a command-driven electronic system, and a hypertext to identify the behavioral components of browsing. In preliminary studies of people in a marketplace, she noted that identifying a unit of focus was difficult (e.g., the object of browsing could be an entire menu or a menu item), that people tended to impose structure on the environment regardless of how unstructured it might be, and that even casual browsing quickly became purposeful as people related the activity to their own interests.

She identified six actions her subjects used while browsing.

(a) Orientation - the need to understand the structure and content of the environment; it continues to evolve as browsing continues.

(b) Place marking - a way to allow users to remember salient objects.

(c) Identification - decisions about the relevance of specific objects.

(d) Resolution of anomalies - browsers' attempts to understand objects that were not clearly identified.

(e) Comparison.

(f) Transition.

It is pertinent to note here that next to last and last actions, respectively, support orientation and identification and allow browsing to progress. This work provides a more user-centered and cognitive approach to browsing than previous work does. A user-centered model of browsing based on the general information-seeking framework that distinguishes different browsing strategies follows. In practice, information seekers use multiple strategies and often use default strategies to initiate search, but this model provides a basis for predicting rational initial strategy selections.

Like all information-seeking activity, browsing is dependent on interactions among the information-seeking factors: task, domain, setting, user characteristics and experience, and system content and interface. Although the higher-order interactions of all the factors influence the specific browsing tactics and behaviors that information seekers select and exhibit, five sets of interactions determine the dimensions that are used to characterise browsing strategies. Two of these dimensions relate to the external and mental representations of the object sought, one is specific to the environment, and two relate to the physical and mental activity of the information seeker:

(a) The domain of the problem and the system mainly determine the external representation of the *object sought.*

(b) The problem and the seeker's knowledge of the domain and the system mainly determine the mental representation of the *object sought.*

(c) The system and the setting determine the degree and type of organisation of information in the *environment.*

(d) The system, the setting, and the seeker's mental models for them mainly determine which browsing strategies are available for application and the *degree of interactivity.*

(e) The setting and the information seeker's past experience and immediate mental and emotional states mainly determine the *cognitive effort,* motivation, and resources used during browsing.

Notably, the object sought during browsing must be considered from two perspectives: the characteristics of the object in the world and the representation of the object in the information seeker's mind. The object may be a well-specified, discrete target (e.g., a book) that can be identified by a single attribute (e.g., a call number). Such objects are well managed by database management systems or string-search techniques. If the single attribute is known by the information seeker (i.e., there is high definition in the user's mental representation), such objects may be immediately recognizable on perception (e.g., known item searches that seek to locate a specific fact or item).

The object may be more general and complex (e.g., a concept or a document) and identifiable by an aggregation of multiple attributes. These objects are typically represented and managed with value-added techniques such as indexing and abstracting. Browsing for these types of objects requires that the information seeker perceive multiple attributes and execute multiple cognitive comparisons and inferences to ascertain pertinence. Objects may also be highly abstract and active (e.g., threads of argumentation in a longitudinal collection of group discussions) and identifiable by a variety of clusters of overlapping attributes. These types of objects may be saved and displayed by various techniques, but are not easily manageable.

Browsing through such objects demands substantial cognitive effort and reflection by the information seeker. The objects of information seeking must also be represented in the mind of the information seeker. Several factors influence these representations. The information problem may be driven by the need to retrieve, to analyze, or to learn and discover; the information seeker has a set amount of domain knowledge, information-seeking experience, personal characteristics, and immediate states of affect; and various setting constraints are active. The object of information seeking may be represented in the seeker's mind as a discrete object with a single attribute (e.g., a date).

Such objects allow the browser simply to compare the objects in the world on this attribute - a task with a small cognitive load. In fact, this sort of problem lends itself to more straightforward retrieval, and browsing may demand considerably more effort by the user. Alternatively, the object can be represented in the browser's mind as a complex concept with multiple attributes. This situation will require more systematic comparisons, more rankings of attribute salience, and thus a greater cognitive load. If the objects are represented as anomalous states of knowledge with many possible attributes that are themselves fuzzy, then the browser must not only make many comparisons and inferences, but also make many interpretations about what may serve as attribute values. The more broadly we decide to browse, the fewer attributes and corresponding objects that we will be willing to admit for careful examination. Furthermore, the attribute values may change as the information seeking progresses, and the information seeker's state of knowledge becomes less fuzzy. Thus, browsing for ill-defined or anomalous objects requires a larger perceptual and cognitive load and more time. It is also possible that information seekers may browse according to a conscious decision to engage in divergent thinking (no object is allowed) or by means of efforts to explore a space to select objects with similar benefits or preferences (choosing one object from many desirable objects). In these cases, as potential objects are perceived during browsing, various levels of cognitive effort may be applied to assess pertinence and determine what action to take next.

Thus, browsing proceeds by comparing the mental representation for the object (an image of the object together with a set of attributes believed to be salient to the search) with the system's representation and altering expectations according to the outcome of each pattern-matching event. The environment is determined by interactions among setting, search system, domain, and task. The environment supports or inhibits browsing according to the level of organisation for the objects represented and by the manner in which feedback is provided. A later section is devoted to the important role that systems play in browsing. For the purpose of defining browsing tactics, the degree of organisation is used as a key dimension. Electronic environments may be characterised by the degree of feedback provided to users. This is the system's perspective of the amount of interactivity, a dimension considered here from the user's perspective. The information seeker is central to all information-seeking activity, and because browsing is a specific case of this activity, the information seeker's personal information infrastructure and the immediate situation influence the browsing. The personal information infrastructure determines whether to browse or use an analytical strategy, what entry point to use, and which tactics to apply as the browsing progresses. The user's emotional state, need, and resources such as time, money, and access privilege influence these decisions, determine whether systematic, opportunistic, or casual approaches will be used, and affect persistence and termination. To define browsing strategies, two dimensions are used here: interactivity and cognitive effort. The interactivity dimension is defined by the number and rate of choices and actions the user makes and takes during information seeking. Low interactivity is indicated by few choices for types of actions and infrequent turn taking.

Cognitive effort refers to the amount of reflection, analysis, integration, and decision making required during browsing. A small cognitive load is indicated by primarily perceptual processing and simple recognition and matching. The types of actions that information seekers exhibit when browsing depend on interactions among the information-seeking factors. From a user-centered, cognitive perspective, tactics and moves are mainly determined by the information seeker's internal representations of the sought object and by expectations about how the process of browsing will proceed. Browsers may expect that comparisons will be based on a simple match of a single attribute or on a match of several attributes. In the case of more open-ended browsing, the experienced browser will expect to draw analogies and make inferences about whether information items found in the system are suitable as attributes for the fuzzy objects of interest. The internal representation of the object of browsing and the expectations about the kinds of matching that will be needed influence the tactics and moves that the information seeker makes during browsing. For example, a single, well-defined attribute that a browser expects to find in a section heading of an article will likely invoke a scanning strategy across section headings.

Note that both types of mental representations change as the browsing progresses. The object becomes more defined according to the attribute specification and frequency of occurrence, and expectations about further progress are informed by reflection on the quality and quantity of attributes represented in the system. For example, consider a novice stock market investor who seeks information on how stock options work and has accessed an electronic discussion archive that provides scrollable subject headings posted by contributors to the discussion. Suppose that the terms *stock* and *option* are attributes that the information seeker expects to match while scrolling.

As the browsing continues, more terms may be added as attributes if those terms occur frequently with *stock* and *option* (e.g., the term, *contract)* or the investor's understanding may grow based on frequent cooccurrences of other concepts such as *option listing, put, call.* These changes are dependent on feedback from the system and the degree of change is a simple indicator for distinguishing systematic, opportunistic, and casual browsing. An interaction between an information seeker and a system that exhibits occasional large changes in the mental representations for the object and the expectations about the process is more clearly opportunistic or casual than is an interaction in which the object and expectations about how matching takes place vary incremen-tally as the search progresses. The behavioral moves exhibited by browsers are manifestations of browsing tactics. The physical actions should be good indicators of cognitive processing because browsing depends on the close coupling of physical, perceptual, and cognitive activity. Four types of browsing strategies are defined: scan, observe, navigate, and monitor.

Two dimensions are used for object: degree of external definition (high means very well defined objects, e.g., simple, concrete data) and degree of definition in the information seeker's mind. External definition is mainly determined by interaction between the domain and search system. The degree of environmental organisation for object representations is the dimension used for scaling the environment. Environmental organisation is mainly determined by interactions among the search system and the setting, with problem and domain to a lesser extent.

The degree of interactivity (high means multiple, rapid turn-taking actions) and amount of cognitive effort (high means considerable reflection, decision making, and analysis while examining objects) are used as dimensions for the information seeker element. Interactivity is determined by interactions among all the information-seeking factors, with domain and outcomes contributing the fewest effects. Cognitive effort is primarily determined by the information seeker's characteristics and the problem, with other factors contributing smaller effects. Clearly, any strategy can be applied to any browsing situation, but efficiency and effectiveness are determined by appropriate applications. Thus, any of the strategies may be used during systematic, opportunistic, or casual browsing.

Scanning is the most basic browsing strategy. It is fundamentally a perceptual recognition activity that compares sets of well-defined objects with an object that is clearly represented in the information seeker's mind. Scanning benefits from highly organised environments that provide clear and concise representations. It can proceed sequentially according to some structural feature of the content, or through some sampling method. Two such tactical approaches are linear and selective scanning.

Linear scanning applies perceptual attention continually and sequentially. For example, information seekers may scan title lists to identity potentially relevant documents to examine, or they may fast-forward through television channels to locate an interesting program. Linear scanning is most applicable to sequential arrangements of similar objects with precise attributes that can be recognised in a single glance, and when the collection is reasonably small or the information seeker is confident about being in the general neighborhood that contains the object. Linear scanning is effective because the eye can recognise simple patterns in as little as 50 milliseconds, although eye movement plus recognition times vary from 125 to 500 ms (Potter and

Levy, 1969). Simon (1979) reports 250-ms fixations for people scanning squares on a chess board. Latencies are shorter when people know where a target will appear (Rayner, 1978), as is the case in linear scanning or reading. A special type of linear scanning is monitoring gauges or controls, and there is evidence that linear sequences of stimuli in a stable position (e.g., reading by fixing on a screen position and having the text move through the position) can dramatically decrease response latency.

Payne and Lang (1991) termed such techniques *rapid communication visual display* and found response latencies with them to be two to three times faster than with spatial displays. However, these speed increases brought severe penalties in error rates that were twice as high as rates with the spatial displays. How these speed and accuracy trade-offs affect scanning tactics for different tasks and how they may be applied to interface design remain to be determined. For example, there is no evidence for how errors of omission or commission affect browsing for textual information, and increased speed benefits may be worth such error penalties in some types of browsing. Errors of omission, for example, may be acceptable when scanning journals or databases to gain the gist of a text. Linear scanning is fatiguing, but the physiological and psychological bounds of scanning in electronic environments have yet to be determined. An alternative to linear scanning is *selective scanning*. This tactic applies perceptual attention according to either an inherent or an imposed stratification of the search space. Most search systems offer some inherent partitions that support selective sampling. For example, information seekers may scan the section headings in a book or the reference lists of different journal articles. This tactic is particularly useful for gaining an overview of content or to identify a neighborhood for linear scanning.

A variation of this tactic is to scan selectively by sampling the search space according to a partitioning rule. Rather than depending on some features or organisations in the search space, random or purposive samples of the search space are identified and scanned for relevance. For example, information seekers may fast forward a videotape 100 feet at a time to locate a particular sequence, or they may examine every first sentence of each screen of text to get a sense of content. The partitioning rule may take advantage of spatial memory and may be particularly useful in locating objects previously seen in the system (e.g., a statement that we believe appears about two-thirds of the way down a left-facing page about one-third of the way through the second chapter of a book). This tactic could be applied to gain an unbiased overview of database coverage or to determine accuracy or integrity.

Sample scanning may also be helpful for discovering promising information neighborhoods in extremely large, unstructured databases. Scanning tactics are most applicable to organised search spaces of reasonable size. What constitutes "reasonable" is often underestimated, especially in electronic environments; nonetheless one of the most obvious ways that electronic search systems can amplify human information-seeking abilities is by emphasising and facilitating scanning tactics. Wiberley and Daugherty (1988) summarised the literature on library patrons' across-document scanning behaviors and suggest that users are willing to scan longer lists of citations from online searches than from OPAC searches and longer lists from electronic than manual systems. They report ranges of 7 to 50 items scanned with few above 20 for manual systems, but occasionally up to 200 for electronic systems. They also note that poor interfaces in electronic systems minimise scanning persistence. It seems plausible that if systems are specifically designed to support scanning rather than simply permit it, users will scan substantial lists of references. There is little evidence on how users scan within electronic documents, although simple affordances such as highlighted query terms and indicators of progress through the document clearly assist within document scanning. Scanning tactics are most useful for tasks for which recognizable and discrete attributes are available. Scanning tactics are most often applied during systematic browsing strategies or for intermediate examinations during opportunistic or casual browsing. One measure of the costs of scanning tactics is attention time, and so research on scanning in electronic environments would be well served by analysing these costs as influenced by different information-seeking factors.

Observational strategies are the most general of all browsing strategies in that they have minimal thresholds for all the browsing dimensions except for cognitive effort. Browsers who use these strategies assume that they are in a promising neighborhood and react to stimuli from that neighborhood. Observational strategies depend on a great deal of parallel input. In busy street scenes, a browser may attend to a variety of sounds, sights, and motions rather than systematically scanning the scene.

Advertisements in newspapers and magazines and provocative titles of books on shelves attract our attention as we passively apply observational tactics. Like scanning, observational strategies are rooted in our physiological and psychological survival instincts and thus are naturally and easily applied as defaults. Observation does require interpretation and reflection to make sense of what is observed and to relate it to information-seeking objectives. Observations may lead to interesting discoveries but yield most initiation control to the environment. For this reason, it is most important for the information seeker to be in a relevant neighborhood. Observations can be executed systematically except for ill-defined objects and fuzzy purposes, for example, regularly reading the morning newspaper or watching a news broadcast. Observation is the primary strategy used in opportunistic and casual browsing because it admits the widest range of objects and unorganised environments.

Serendipitous observations are lauded as a benefit of browsing, but they occur as a result of reflection and association rather than simple perception and pattern matching. Interfaces that support observational strategies should provide alternative views of information. Because observational strategies yield significant control to the environment, information should be clearly represented and demarcated. Alternative representations should be available for the user to transform so that pattern recognition may lead to association and reflection.

The *navigation* strategy balances the influence of the user and the environment. The environment constrains browsing by providing possible routes, and the user exercises some control by selecting which routes to follow. *Navigation* is a term that is used broadly and differently in the literature. In much of the human-computer interaction literature, navigation is considered to be synonymous with browsing rather than one of several specific browsing strategies.

One model that does distinguish between browsing and navigation was proposed by Waterworth and Chignell (1991). Their model of information exploration distinguishes querying and browsing, object specification (command interaction styles) and object recognition (menu interaction styles), and navigation from mediation. In their model, navigation is taken to mean a high degree of user control with mediation depending more on system control.

Physical navigation is often used as a metaphor for traversing of a hypertext or a database. The activity that users engage in as they follow links in a hypertext is the navigation that we consider to be a browsing strategy. In this strategy, the process and the information found along the way are what is important. A better metaphor for this strategy may be "grazing" or "berry picking" (Bates, 1989), but the activity is commonly called *navigation* in the human-computer interaction and hypertext literature and so is adopted here. This type of navigation is in contrast with the goal-oriented physical navigation that uses cues from the environment only to check progress toward the goal. In physical navigation, the object sought is most often a predetermined destination, and the process is adjusting course according to attributes (conditions) provided by the environment. Navigation connotes goal-oriented behavior in which plans and subplans respond to the environment. This dynamic interplay between navigator and environment is what makes navigation a popular metaphor for human-computer interaction.

Navigation is a useful name for a browsing strategy in so far as it denotes observations of the environment and adjustments in behavior based on these observations. It is, however, a weak metaphor for browsing through an information space, in two respects: The destination for information seeking is seldom predetermined - intellectual space is highly amorphous, and much of what is called navigation involves problem definition and clarification. Second, information-seeking activity draws information to the information seeker rather than transporting the information seeker to the information. This is especially true of electronic environments, in which we remain physically stationary and gather information to our screen rather than travel to some location and idea. Using navigation as a global metaphor for browsing admits the side effects of becoming lost. In electronic systems this effect has been most often referred to as lost in hyperspace (Nielsen, 1990a).

It is useful to distinguish between being lost and confused as a result of the environment (e.g., poor maps or bad road signs in physical space, and poor interfaces in information space) and being lost or confused as a result of the information problem (i.e., being lost in one's own mind). Although it is likely that improved interfaces (e.g., graphic maps, place markers, organisational labels and cues) will minimise disorientation caused by the system, being lost in a collection of thoughts will remain a human problem regardless of system advances. This point of view, that is, understanding content (mental orientation) is more critical than system orientation, was reinforced by two investigations we conducted to determine the effects of blatant metaphors on learning. Two versions of a hypertext explanation of the information-seeking framework were prepared using the GUIDE system. One version, called the *jump* implementation, reinforced the navigation metaphor. The screen consisted of a single text window, with link anchors immediately followed by the word *jump* in boldface uppercase letters. Clicking on the link anchor replaced the text with the text in the linked node. The other implementation, called the *bring* version, reinforced the metaphor of bringing information to the screen rather than jumping to it. Link anchors were immediately followed by the word *bring* in boldface uppercase letters. Clicking on the link anchor opened a new window that overlapped the active window immediately below the anchor. Forty-eight library and information science students were randomly assigned to one of the two conditions. They received mouse training and training in their assigned linking mechanism, during which time the metaphor was verbally reinforced. They then were given 30 minutes to study the database. After their study period, the subjects were given a written test to determine their understanding, asked to draw a diagram of the organisational structure of the database, completed a questionnaire, and participated in a focus group discussion.

No statistically reliable differences were found between the groups, and there was wide variance on all indicators within the groups. The study was replicated the following semester with a third condition of a linear electronic version of the database added. The results of that study were similar to those of the first study. In both cases, reports of disorientation were not correlated with other results or any of the main treatments. Apparently, the metaphor was not so important to performance as the users' abilities and the complexity of the content. Navigation as a browsing strategy refers to the ongoing observation of environmental attributes, adjustments to the mental problem representation based on these observations, and the resulting behavioral actions.

Navigation is thus information seeking that proceeds incrementally based on feedback from the information system. The ways in which the system provides feedback is a critical factor in navigation.

Different systems provide distinct levels of navigational freedom, ranging from highly systematic, mandatory paths to absolutely no guidance whatsoever. Successful systems fall somewhere in between, offering some choice to users but suggesting directions and providing informative cues about progress. Systems that provide explicit hypertextual links support more systematic browsing strategies, and those that provide implicit links support more exploratory or casual browsing.

This strategy is most clearly supported by the structural layouts of museums. Navigation has become an important (but weak) metaphor for electronic systems and is the principal inspiration for static hypertexts. In one navigation variation, users are invited to follow paths through the database by selecting one of possibly many links from a current node to other nodes. Thus, the tactics used are simple selections from the choices active on the path. Navigation strategies can be applied casually or systematically, although they depend on taking advantage of existing links or the user's ability to create new links. Navigation is an attractive compromise between user and system responsibility because the system invites or suggests links to follow but the user is free to choose from among many links or continue in linear fashion.

A *monitor* strategy is often applied in conjunction with systematic browsing or other primary activities such as reading. Monitoring is most similar to scanning except that it tolerates poorly structured environments. For example, while reading text related to a specific topic, a monitor browsing strategy "listens" for concepts related to another topic of interest. Professionals in any field often automatically apply the monitor strategy by spontaneously relating to their own field what they read in an unrelated area. It is this strategy that is perhaps most important to discovery and creative connections among disparate ideas, and it is the reason that scholars revere serendipity. Although this strategy may be partly subconscious, it depends on the user's making associations among concepts in the mind and representations in the information space.

6

TELNET: A Modern Way of Communication

"Civilization is always in danger when those who have never learned to obey are given the right to command."

—Bishcp F.J. Sheen

The term *telnet* also refers to software which implements the client part of the protocol. TELNET clients have been available on most Unix systems for many years and are available for virtually all platforms. Most network equipment and OSs with a TCP/IP stack support some kind of TELNET service server for their remote configuration (including ones based on Windows NT). Recently, SSH has begun to dominate remote access for Unix-based machines.

"To telnet" is also used as a verb meaning to establish or use a TELNET or other interactive TCP connection, as in, "To change your password, telnet to the server and run the passwd command".

Most often, a user will be *telneting* to a unix-like server system or a simple network device such as a switch. For example, a user might "telnet in from home to check his mail at school". In doing so, he would be using a telnet client to connect from his computer to one of his servers.

Once the connection is established, he would then log in with his account information and execute operating system commands remotely on that computer, such as *ls* or *cd*.

On many systems, the client may also be used to make interactive raw-TCP sessions.

Security

When TELNET was initially developed in 1969, most users of networked computers were in the computer departments of academic institutions, or at large private and government research facilities. In this environment, security was not nearly as much of a concern as it became after the bandwidth explosion of the 1990s. The rise in the number of people with access to the Internet, and by extension, the number of people attempting to hack into other people's servers made encrypted alternatives much more necessary.

Experts in computer security, such as SANS Institute, and the members of the comp.os.linux.security newsgroup recommend that the use of TELNET for remote logins should be discontinued under all normal circumstances, for the following reasons:

- TELNET, by default, does not encrypt any data sent over the connection (including passwords), and so it is trivial to eavesdrop on the communications and use the password later for malicious purposes; anybody who has access to a router, switch, or gateway located on the network between the two hosts where TELNET is being used can intercept the packets passing by and easily obtain login and password information (and whatever else is typed) with any of several common utilities like tcpdump and Wireshark.

- Most implementations of TELNET lack an authentication scheme that makes it possible to ensure that communication is carried out between the two desired hosts, and not intercepted in the middle.
- Commonly used TELNET daemons have several vulnerabilities discovered over the years.

These security-related shortcomings have seen the usage of the TELNET protocol drop rapidly, especially on the public Internet, in favor of a more secure and functional protocol called SSH, first released in 1995. SSH provides all functionality of telnet, with the addition of strong encryption to prevent sensitive data such as passwords from being intercepted, and public key authentication, to ensure that the remote computer is actually who it claims to be. As has happened with other early Internet protocols, extensions to the TELNET protocol provide TLS security and SASL authentication that address the above issues. However, most TELNET implementations do not support these extensions; and there has been relatively little interest in implementing these as SSH is adequate for most purposes. The main advantage of TLS-TELNET would be the ability to use certificate-authority signed server certificates to authenticate a server host to a client that does not yet have the server key stored. In SSH, there is a weakness in that the user must trust the first session to a host when it has not yet acquired the server key.

Advance Status

As of the mid-2000s, while the TELNET protocol itself has been mostly superseded, TELNET clients are still used, usually when diagnosing problems, to manually "talk" to other services without specialized client software. For example, it is sometimes used in debugging network services such as an SMTP or HTTP server, by serving as a simple way to send commands to the server and examine the responses.

On UNIX, though, other software such as *nc* (netcat) or *socat* are finding greater favor with some system administrators for testing purposes, as they can be called with arguments to not send any terminal control handshaking data.

TELNET is still very popular in enterprise networks to access host applications, i.e. on IBM Mainframes.

TELNET is also heavily used for MUD games played over the Internet, as well as talkers, MUSH es, MUCKs, MOOes, and the resurgent BBS community. By using image-to-ASCII algorithms, it can also be used for primitive "video" streaming. Recently, ASCII-WM offered live broadcasts of the 2006 World Cup.

TELNET can also be used as a rudimentary IRC client if one knows the protocol well enough.

In the 2007 Microsoft Windows release, Windows Vista, Telnet.exe is no longer installed by default, but is still included as an installable feature.

Details of Protocol

TELNET is a client-server protocol, based on a reliable connection-oriented transport. Typically this is TCP port 23, although TELNET predates TCP/IP and was originally run on NCP. The protocol has many extensions, some of which have been adopted as Internet Standards. IETF standards STD 27 through STD 32 define various extensions, most of which are extremely common. Other extensions are on the IETF standards track as proposed standards.

TELNET Clients

Multiplatform

- PuTTY is a free SSH, TELNET, rlogin, and raw TCP client for Windows, Linux, and Unix.
- mTelnet is a free full-screen TELNET client for Windows & OS/2. Easy to use client with Zmodem download capability.
- Twisted Conch includes a telnet client/server implementation.
- IVT is a free multisession TELNET client for Windows & DOS. Also supports SSH and Kerberos (not free). Includes useful features like auto-login and scripting.
- SyncTERM is a free open-source TELNET/RLogin/SSH client/terminal for Windows and nix platforms with windowed/full-screen and Zmodem support.

Macintosh

- tn3270 is a free TELNET client for Macintosh designed to work with IBM mainframe systems that use the TN3270 protocol.
- Terminal is a TELNET capable command line interface application that comes as part of all versions of Macintosh OS X.
- NiftyTelnet is a small Telnet client for older MacOS versions that also support SSH.
- dataComet is a full-featured Telnet & SSH application for the Macintosh.

Windows

- z/Scope Express VT is a telnet/SSH client for Windows.

- AbsoluteTelnet is a client for all versions of Windows, and includes telnet, SSH1, and SSH2.
- Hyperterminal Private Edition is another Windows telnet client, free for personal use.
- TeraTerm is a free telnet/SSH client for Windows that offers more features than the built-in telnet as well as offering a free SSH plug-in.
- TN3270 Plus is a telnet/SSH client for Windows.
- Windows comes with a built in telnet client, accessible from the command prompt.

Free with Source Code

- dtelnet is a free TELNET client for Windows.
- Pueblo/UE is a free TELNET client for Windows with support for in-line HTML.
- Console telnet is a full screen (console) TELNET client for MS Win32 environments.

Non-free Source Code

- Whitehorn Secure Terminal free TELNET client for Windows.
- Simpterm is a Unicode savy TELNET client for MS Win32 environments that for example can be used for Chinese.
- SimpleMU is a shareware TELNET client.
- CRT and SecureCRT are TELNET clients with scripting capabilities in VBScript, Javascript and Perl.

TELNET Servers

Free with Source Code

- telnetd is an embeddable TELNET daemon written in Java.

- Poor Woman's Telnet Server is a standalone java TELNET server which bases upon telnetd.
- Synchronet is a Win32 and Linux BBS Server that also supports http, nntp, pop3, ftp and other protocols.

Related RFCs

- RFC 854 TELNET protocol specification
- RFC 855 TELNET option specifications
- RFC 856 TELNET binary transmission
- RFC 857 TELNET echo option
- RFC 858 TELNET suppress Go Ahead option
- RFC 859 TELNET status option
- RFC 860 TELNET timing mark option
- RFC 861 TELNET extended options - list option
- RFC 885 Telnet end of record option
- RFC 1041 Telnet 3270 regime option
- RFC 1079 Telnet terminal speed option
- RFC 1091 Telnet terminal-type option
- RFC 1096 Telnet X display location option
- RFC 1097 Telnet subliminal-message option
- RFC 1205 5250 Telnet interface
- RFC 1372 Telnet remote flow control option
- RFC 2941 Telnet Authentication Option
- RFC 2942 Telnet Authentication: Kerberos Version 5
- RFC 2943 TELNET Authentication Using DSA
- RFC 2944 Telnet Authentication: SRP
- RFC 2946 Telnet Data Encryption Option
- RFC 4248 The telnet URI Scheme
- RFC 4777 IBM's iSeries Telnet Enhancements

7

Usenet

Usenet is one of the oldest computer network communications systems still in widespread use. It was established in 1980, following experiments from the previous year, over a decade before the World Wide Web was introduced and the general public got access to the Internet. It was originally conceived as a "poor man's ARPANET," employing UUCP to offer mail and file transfers, as well as announcements through the newly developed news software. This system, developed at University of North Carolina at Chapel Hill and Duke University, was called USENET to emphasize its creators' hope that the USENIX organization would take an active role in its operation (Daniel *et al*, 1980). The articles that users post to Usenet are organized into topical categories called newsgroups, which are themselves logically organized into hierarchies of subjects. For instance, sci.math and sci.physics are within the sci hierarchy, for science. When a user subscribes to a newsgroup, the news client software keeps track of which articles that user has read. In most newsgroups, the majority of the articles are responses to some other article. The set of articles which can be traced to one single non-reply article is called a thread. Most modern newsreaders display the articles arranged into threads and subthreads, making it easy to follow a single discussion in a high-volume newsgroup. When a user posts an article, it is initially only available on that user's news server. Each news server, however, talks to one or more other servers (its "newsfeeds") and exchanges articles with them. In this fashion, the article is copied from server to server and (if all goes well) eventually reaches every server in the network. The later peer-to-peer networks operate on a similar principle; but for Usenet it is normally the sender, rather than the receiver, who initiates transfers. Some have noted that this seems a monstrously inefficient protocol in the era of abundant high-speed network access. Usenet was designed for a time when networks were much slower, and not always available. Many sites on the original Usenet network would connect only once or twice a day to batch-transfer messages in and out.

Usenet has significant cultural importance in the networked world, having given rise to, or popularized, many widely recognized concepts and terms such as "FAQ" and "spam." Today, almost all Usenet traffic is carried over the Internet. The current format and transmission of Usenet articles is very similar to that of Internet email messages. However, Usenet articles are posted for general consumption; any usenet user has access to all newsgroups, unlike email, which requires a list of known recipients. Today, Usenet has diminished in importance with respect to mailing lists, web forums and weblogs. The difference, though, is that Usenet requires no personal registration with the group concerned, that information need not be stored on a remote server, that archives are always available, and that reading the messages requires not a mail or web client, but a news client.

Newsreader Clients

Newsgroups are typically accessed with special client software that connects to a news server. With the rise of the world wide web, web front-ends have sometimes been used to access newsgroups via the aforementioned news-to-web gateways. However, these gateways often provide limited features, and for that reason using a local client is still regarded as the best way to access newsgroups.

Newsreader clients are available for all major operating systems and come in all shapes and sizes. Mail clients or "communication suites" also now commonly have an integrated newsreader. Often, however, these integrated clients are of low quality, e.g. incorrectly implementing Usenet protocols, standards and conventions. Many of these integrated clients, for example the one in Microsoft's Outlook Express, are disliked by purists because of their misbehavior.

Moderated and Unmoderated Newsgroups

A minority of newsgroups are moderated. That means that messages submitted by readers are not distributed to USENET, but instead are emailed to the moderators of the newsgroup, for approval. Moderated newsgroups have rules called charters. Moderators are persons whose job is to ensure that messages that the readers see in newsgroups conform to the charter of the newsgroup. Typically, moderators are appointed in the proposal for the newsgroup, and changes of moderators follow a succession plan.

The job of the moderator is to receive submitted articles, review them, and inject approved articles so that they can be properly propagated worldwide. Such articles must bear the Approved: header line.

Unmoderated newsgroups form the majority of USENET newsgroups, and messages submitted by readers for unmoderated newsgroups are immediately propagated for everyone to see.

Creation of moderated newsgroups often becomes a hot subject of controversy, raising issues regarding censorship and the desire of a subset of users to form an intentional community.

ISPs, News Servers, and Newsfeeds

Many Internet service providers, and many other Internet sites, operate news servers for their users to access. ISPs that do not operate their own servers directly will often offer their users an account from another provider that specifically operates newsfeeds. Most commonly, these accounts are through Supernews, Giganews and Usenet.com. Usually the ISP will get a kickback for referring the customer to the Usenet provider. In early news implementations, the server and newsreader were a single program suite, running on the same system. Today, one uses separate newsreader client software, a program that resembles an email client but accesses Usenet servers instead.

Not all ISPs run news servers. A news server is one of the most difficult Internet services to administer well because of the large amount of data involved, small customer base (compared to mainstream Internet services such as email and web access), and a disproportionately high volume of customer support incidents (frequently complaining of missing news articles that are not the ISP's fault). Some ISPs outsource news operation to specialist sites, which will usually appear to a user as though the ISP ran the server itself. Many sites carry a restricted newsfeed, with a limited number of newsgroups. Commonly omitted from such a newsfeed are foreign-language newsgroups and the alt.binaries hierarchy which largely carries software, music, videos and images, and accounts for over 99 percent of article data.

For those who have access to the Internet, but do not have access to a news server, Google Groups allows reading and posting of text news groups via the World Wide Web. Though this or other "news-to-Web gateways" are not always as easy to use as specialized newsreader software—especially when threads get long—they are often much easier to search. Users who lack access to an ISP news server can use Google Groups to access the alt.free.newsservers newsgroup, which has information about open news servers.

There are also Usenet providers that specialize in offering service to users whose ISPs do not carry news, or that carry a restricted feed. One list of such providers is available at UsenetProviders' list of Usenet providers (Germany) or Jeremy Nixon's list of (paid) Usenet providers.

Technical Details

Usenet is a set of protocols for generating, storing and retrieving news "articles" (which resemble Internet mail messages) and for exchanging them among a readership which is potentially widely distributed. These protocols most commonly use a flooding algorithm which propagates copies throughout a network of participating servers. Whenever a message reaches a server, that server forwards the message to all its network neighbors that haven't yet seen the article. Only one copy of a message is stored per server, and each server makes it available on demand to the (typically local) readers able to access that server. Usenet was thus one of the first peer-to-peer applications, although in this case the "peers" are themselves servers that the users then access, rather than the users themselves being peers on the network.

RFC 850 was the first formal specification of the messages exchanged by Usenet servers. It was superseded by RFC

1036. One difference between Usenet and newer peer-to-peer applications is that one can request the automated removal of a posting from the whole network by creating a cancel message, although due to a lack of authentication and resultant abuse, this capability is frequently disabled.

Copyright holders may still request the manual deletion of infringing material using the provisions of World Intellectual Property Organization treaty implementations, such as the U.S. Online Copyright Infringement Liability Limitation Act. On the Internet, Usenet is typically on TCP Port 119.

Web Interfaces

With the rising popularity of the World Wide Web, so have arisen many Web-to-Usenet gateways. These interfaces are seen as controversial by some Usenet users. Google Groups is usually cited as a prime example of what can go wrong with Web-to-Usenet gateways, since it is the most popular and largest such service. However, the criticism also applies to many other such gateways in principle.

Since February 2001 Google Groups has provided a web interface to Usenet newsgroups. It also allows the creation of mailing lists like Yahoo! Groups. In early 2007 Google Groups moved to a new "Web 2.0" interface with more icons, larger type and an America On-Line type interface. While seemingly deployed to improve the accessiblity of USENET the new interface has been widely (indeed nearly universally) disparaged for both its reduced usability and its utility.

One of many concerns that have been expressed about the Google interface is that novices may have difficulty realising that they are participating in a Usenet newsgroup rather than in a web forum hosted by Google. Google

Groups is not very outspoken about the fact and doesn't make it very clear in the web interface that some of the groups at Google Groups are Usenet groups, while others are local Google-only groups.

Other concerns are:

1. Web-to-Usenet gateways provide a service for e-mail spammers, since a spammer's web spider can now also extract e-mail addresses from Usenet postings without any additional effort. Before such gateways, an e-mail spammer would have to use a separate tool to gain access to a news feed (as Usenet spammers do). Since 2005, Google Groups tries to prevent e-mail address harvesting by scrambling the display of e-mail addresses on their web pages.
2. Web-to-Usenet gateways often hide the fact from users that they are actually on Usenet, and that it would be a good idea to learn and follow Usenet customs and established rules. They further hide the fact that Usenet is still at its core a decentralized store-and-forward system and, therefore, articles do not simply appear "everywhere" once they have been posted. This typically leads to multiple posts with the same contents and/or expressed dissatisfaction about why there are no answers within minutes and/or why there are multiple answers which essentially say the same thing.
3. Web-to-Usenet gateways often cut away or hide "overhead" information (e.g. header information like message IDs) or, even worse, signatures. This leaves Web-users puzzled about what people are talking about when they write things like "See my sig" or "See msgid ...".

4. Web-to-Usenet gateways typically provide fewer features than conventional News Reader software. For example, the ability to filter (users, subject lines, etc.), to sort threads in multiple ways, draft articles, etc., is typically missing.
5. Web-to-Usenet gateways are often very badly policed. Post 2006, this is typical not only of such gateways, but also many feed providers. Abusive behavior from the Web-to-Usenet gateway users in some newsgroups is now legendary, and the operators have not yet mustered the will and/or resources to effectively keep a lid on abusive users. Automated complaint systems seldom result in any action.
6. Web-to-Usenet gateways enable less technically savvy people to enter Usenet. These people tend to be less familiar with the Usenet system and Usenet etiquette, and can cause annoyance for other users.
7. Web-to-Usenet gateways lower the entry barrier to Usenet. The slightly higher entry requirements, and the degree of obscurity Usenet possesses required users to have a higher level of knowledge and capability and as such tended to exclude those who were not at least mildly computer savvy, which in turn had the effect of tending to guarantee at least a minimum level of education, which in turn, overall, tended to ensure at least a minimum level of decency in behaviour. This is not an iron rule of course, but merely a tendency overall, which of course when applied to millions of people, had a profound effect on the overall culture of Usenet.
8. Web-to-Usenet gateways often offer a searchable archive. One of the advantages of Usenet was that posters knew their material was only being read by

the readership of their group and would, in a week or two, have disappeared forever. This particular type of semi-public, semi-private conversation was unusual and very useful.

On the positive side:

1. Web-to-Usenet gateways lower the entry barrier to Usenet, making it easier for non-technical people to become involved.
2. Web-to-Usenet gateways often offer a searchable archive, making the vast amount of knowledge in Usenet more easily accessible.

Organization

The major set of worldwide newsgroups is contained within nine hierarchies, eight of which are operated under consensual guidelines that govern their administration and naming.

Binary Content

Usenet was originally created to distribute text content encoded in the 7-bit ASCII character set. With the help of programs that encode 8-bit values into ASCII, it became practical to distribute binary files content.

Binary posts, due to their size and dubious copyright status, were in time restricted to specific newsgroups, making it easier for administrators to allow or disallow the traffic. The oldest widely used encoding method is uuencode, from the Unix uucp package. In the late 1980s Usenet articles were often limited to 60,000 characters, and larger hard limits exist today. Files are therefore commonly split into sections that require reassembly by the reader. With the header extensions and the Base64 and Quoted-Printable

MIME encodings, there was a new generation of binary transport. In practice, MIME has seen increased adoption in text messages, but it is avoided for most binary attachments. Some operating systems with metadata attached to files use specialized encoding formats.

For Mac OS, both Binhex and special MIME types are used. Other lesser known encoding systems that may have been used at one time were BTOA, XX encoding, BOO, and USR encoding.

In an attempt to reduce file transfer times, an informal file encoding known as yEnc was introduced in 2001. It achieves about a 30% reduction in data transferred by assuming that most 8-bit characters can safely be transferred across the network without first encoding into the 7-bit ASCII space.

The standard method of uploading binary content to Usenet is to first archive the files into RAR archives (for large files usually in 20 MB or 50 MB parts) then create Parchive files. Parity files are used to recreate missing data. This is needed often, as not every part of the files reach a server. These are all then encoded into yEnc and uploaded to the selected binary groups.

Newsgroup experiments first occurred in 1979. Tom Truscott and Jim Ellis of Duke University came up with the idea as a replacement for a local announcement program, and established a link with nearby University of North Carolina using Bourne shell scripts written by Steve Bellovin. The public release of news was in the form of conventional compiled software, written by Steve Daniel and Truscott.

UUCP networks spread quickly due to the lower costs involved, and the ability to use existing leased lines, X.25

links or even ARPANET connections. By 1983 the number of UUCP hosts had grown to 550, nearly doubling to 940 in 1984.

As the mesh of UUCP hosts rapidly expanded, it became desirable to distinguish the Usenet subset from the overall network. A vote was taken at the 1982 USENIX conference to choose a new name. The name Usenet was retained, but it was established that it only applied to news. The name UUCPNET became the common name for the overall network.

In addition to UUCP, early Usenet traffic was also exchanged with Fidonet and other dial-up BBS networks. Widespread use of Usenet by the BBS community was facilitated by the introduction of UUCP feeds made possible by MS-DOS implementations of UUCP such as UFGATE (UUCP to FidoNet Gateway), FSUUCP and UUPC. The Network News Transfer Protocol, or NNTP, was introduced in 1985 to distribute Usenet articles over TCP/IP as a more flexible alternative to informal Internet transfers of UUCP traffic. Since the Internet boom of the 1990s, almost all Usenet distribution is over NNTP, rendering obsolete the earlier dictum that "Usenet is not the Internet."

Early versions of Usenet used Duke's A News software. At Berkeley an improved version called B News was produced by Matt Glickman and Mark Horton. With a message format that offered compatibility with Internet mail and improved performance, it became the dominant server software. C News, developed by Geoff Collyer and Henry Spencer at the University of Toronto, was comparable to B News in features but offered considerably faster processing. In the early 1990s, InterNetNews by Rich Salz was developed to take advantage of the continuous message flow made possible by NNTP versus the batched store-and-forward design of UUCP. Since that time INN development has continued, and other news server software has also been developed.

Usenet was the initial Internet community and the place for many of the most important public developments in the commercial Internet. It was the place where Tim Berners-Lee announced the launch of the World Wide Web, and Marc Andreesen announced the creation of the Mosaic browser and the introduction of the image tag, which revolutionized the World Wide Web by turning it into a graphical medium.

Web-based archiving of Usenet posts began in 1995 at Deja News with a very large, searchable database. In 2001, this database was acquired by Google.

AOL announced that it would discontinue its integrated Usenet service in early 2005, citing the growing popularity of weblogs, chat forums and on-line conferencing. The AOL community had a tremendous role in popularizing the Usenet some 11 years earlier, with all of its positive and negative aspects. This change marked the end of the legendary Eternal September. Others, however, feel that Google Groups, especially with its new user interface, has picked up the torch that AOL has dropped—and that Eternal September has yet to end. Over time, the amount of Usenet traffic has steadily increased. It is important to note, however, that much of this traffic increase reflects not an increase in discrete users or newsgroup discussions, but instead the combination of massive automated spamming and an increase in the use of *.binaries* newsgroups in which large files (frequently pornography or pirated media) are often posted publicly.

Many terms now in common use on the Internet—so-called "jargon"—originated or were popularized on Usenet.

Likewise, many conflicts which later spread to the rest of the Internet, such as the ongoing difficulties over spamming, began on Usenet.

Google Groups hosts an archive of Usenet posts dating back to May 1981. The archive was originally started by a company called DejaNews (later only Deja), purchased by Google in February 2001. A Usenet Timeline is provided in the Help section. Already during the DejaNews era the archive had become a popular constant in Usenet culture, and remains so today.

However, there are two main issues people have with Google Groups and similar services:

1. Fear of loss of privacy. An archive simplifies ways to profile people. This has partly been countered with the introduction of the non-standard *X-No-Archive: Yes* header, which is itself seen as controversial.
2. The web interface.

Note that there are two distinct types of "Google Groups", namely traditional Usenet groups and Google internal groups that can only be accessed from Google. The Google user interface and documentation does not make the distinction clear, which is probably deliberate.

8

Internet and Information Technology

> "The trouble with Golden Rule is that before most men are ready to live by it they have lead in their legs and silver in their hair."

Internet and email are now widely popular modes of media.

Here in this chapter we are giving an introduction of it. The Internet links are computer networks all over the world so that users can share resources and communicate with each other. Some computers, have direct access to all the facilities on the Internet such as the universities. And other computers, e.g. privately-owned ones, have indirect links through a commercial service provider, who offers some or all of the Internet facilities. In order to be connected to Internet, you must go through service suppliers. Many options are offered with monthly rates. Depending on the option chosen, access time may vary. The Internet is what we call a metanetwork, that is, a network of networks that spans the globe. It's impossible to give an exact count of the number of networks or users that comprise the Internet, but it is easily in the thousands and millions respectively. The Internet employs a set of standardized protocols which allow for the sharing of resources among different kinds of computers that communicate with each other on the network.

These standards, sometimes referred to as the Internet Protocol Suite, are the rules that developers adhere to when creating new functions for the Internet. The Internet is also what we call a distributed system; there is no central archives. Technically, no one runs the Internet. Rather, the Internet is made up of thousands of smaller networks. The Internet thrives and develops as its many users find new ways to create, display and retrieve the information that constitutes the Internet.

In its infancy, the Internet was originally conceived by the Department of Defense as a way to protect government communications systems in the event of a military strike. The original network, dubbed ARPANet (for the Advanced Research Projects Agency that developed it) evolved into a communications channel among contractors, military personnel, and university researchers who were contributing to ARPA projects.

The network employed a set of standard protocols to create an effective way for these people to communicate and share data with each other.

ARPAnet's popularity continued to spread among researchers, and in the 1980's the National Science Foundation, whose NSFNet, linked several high speed computers, took charge of the what had come to be known as the Internet. By the late 1980's, thousands of cooperating networks were participating in the Internet.

In 1991, the U.S. High Performance Computing Act established the NREN (National Research & Education Network). NREN's goal was to develop and maintain high-speed networks for research and education, and to investigate commercial uses for the Internet.

The rest, as they say, is history in the making. The Internet has been improved through the developments of such services as Gopher and the World Wide Web.

Even though the Internet is predominantly thought of as a research oriented network, it continues to grow as an informational, creative, and commercial resource every day and all over the world.

The first TCP/IP-wide area network was operational by January 1, 1983, when the United States' National Science Foundation (NSF) constructed a university network backbone that would later become the NSFNet. (This date is held by some to be technically that of the birth of the Internet.) It was then followed by the opening of the network to commercial interests in 1985. Important, separate networks that offered gateways into, then later merged with, the NSFNet include Usenet, BITNET and the various commercial and educational networks, such as X.25, Compuserve and JANET. Telenet (later called Sprintnet) was a large privately-funded national computer network with free dial-up access in cities throughout the U.S. that had been in operation since the 1970s. This network eventually merged with the others in the 1990s as the TCP/IP protocol became increasingly popular. The ability of TCP/IP to work over these pre-existing communication networks, especially the international X.25 IPSS network, allowed for a great ease of growth. Use of the term "Internet" to describe a single global TCP/IP network originated around this time. The network gained a public face in the 1990s. On August 6, 1991, CERN, which straddles the border between France and Switzerland, publicized the new World Wide Web project, two years after Tim Berners-Lee had begun creating HTML, HTTP and the first few Web pages at CERN.

An early popular web browser was *ViolaWWW* based upon HyperCard. It was eventually replaced in popularity by the Mosaic web browser. In 1993 the National Center for Supercomputing Applications at the University of Illinois released version 1.0 of *Mosaic*, and by late 1994 there was growing public interest in the previously academic/technical Internet. By 1996 the word "Internet" was coming into common daily usage, frequently misused to refer to the World Wide Web.

Meanwhile, over the course of the decade, the Internet successfully accommodated the majority of previously existing public computer networks (although some networks, such as FidoNet, have remained separate). According to a research done by K.G. Coffman and Andrew Odlyzko, the internet is growing at a rate of over 100% per year. This growth is often attributed to the lack of central administration, which allows organic growth of the network, as well as the non-proprietary open nature of the Internet protocols, which encourages vendor interoperability and prevents any one company from exerting too much control over the network.

Common Uses of the Internet

E-mail

The concept of sending electronic text messages between parties in a way analogous to mailing letters or memos predates the creation of the Internet. Even today it can be important to distinguish between Internet and internal e-mail systems. Internet e-mail may travel and be stored unencrypted on many other networks and machines out of both the sender's and the recipient's control. During this time it is quite possible for the content to be read and even tampered with by third parties, if anyone considers it important enough. Purely internal or intranet mail systems, where the information never leaves the corporate or organization's network, are much more secure, although in any organization there will be IT and other personnel whose job may involve monitoring, and occasionally accessing, the email of other employees not addressed to them. Web-based email (webmail) between parties on the same webmail system may not actually 'go' anywhere—it merely sits on the one server and is tagged in various ways so as to appear in one person's 'sent items' list and in others' 'in boxes' or other 'folders' when viewed.

The World Wide Web

Through keyword-driven Internet research using search engines, like Google, millions worldwide have easy, instant access to a vast and diverse amount of online information. Compared to encyclopedias and traditional libraries, the World Wide Web has enabled a sudden and extreme decentralization of information and data. Many individuals and some companies and groups have adopted the use of "Web logs" or blogs, which are largely used as easily-updatable online diaries. Some commercial organizations encourage staff to fill them with advice on their areas of specialization in the hope that visitors will be impressed by the expert knowledge and free information, and be attracted to the corporation as a result.

One example of this practice is Microsoft, whose product developers publish their personal blogs in order to pique the public's interest in their work. For more information on the distinction between the World Wide Web and the Internet itself—as in everyday use the two are sometimes confused.

Remote access

Basically, the Internet allows computer users to connect to other computers and information stores easily, wherever they may be across the world. They may do this with or without the use of security, authentication and encryption technologies, depending on the requirements. This is encouraging new ways of working from home, collaboration and information sharing in many industries. An accountant sitting at home can audit the books of a company based in another country, on a server situated in a third country that is remotely maintained by IT specialists in a fourth.

These accounts could have been created by home-working book-keepers, in other remote locations, based on information e-mailed to them from offices all over the world. Some of these things were possible before the widespread use of the Internet, but the cost of private, leased lines would have made many of them infeasible in practice. An office worker away from his desk, perhaps the other side of the world on a business trip or a holiday, can open a remote desktop session into their normal office PC using a secure Virtual Private Network (VPN) connection via the Internet.

This gives the worker complete access to all of their normal files and data, including e-mail and other applications, while away from the office. This concept is also referred to by some network security people as the Virtual Private Nightmare, because it extends the secure perimeter of a corporate network into its employees' homes; this has been the source of some notable security breaches, but also provides security for the workers.

Collaboration

The low-cost and nearly instantaneous sharing of ideas, knowledge, and skills has made collaborative work dramatically easier. Not only can a group cheaply communicate and test, but the wide reach of the Internet allows such groups to easily form in the first place, even among niche interests. An example of this is the free software movement in software development which produced GNU and Linux from scratch and has taken over development of Mozilla and OpenOffice.org (formerly known as Netscape Communicator and StarOffice). Internet 'chat', whether in the form of IRC 'chat rooms' or channels, or via instant messaging systems allow colleagues to stay in touch in a very convenient way when working at their computers during the day. Messages can be sent and viewed even more quickly and conveniently than via e-mail.

Extension to these systems may allow files to be exchanged, 'whiteboard' drawings to be shared as well as voice and video contact between team members. Version control systems allow collaborating teams to work on shared sets of documents without either accidentally overwriting each other's work or having members wait until they get 'sent' documents to be able to add their thoughts and changes.

File Sharing

A computer file can be e-mailed to customers, colleagues and friends as an attachment. It can be uploaded to a Web site or FTP server for easy download by others. It can be put into a "shared location" or onto a file server for instant use by colleagues. The load of bulk downloads to many users can be eased by the use of "mirror" servers or peer-to-peer networks. In any of these cases, access to the file may be controlled by user authentication; the transit of the file over the Internet may be obscured by encryption and money may change hands before or after access to the file is given.

The price can be paid by the remote charging of funds from, for example a credit card whose details are also passed—hopefully fully encrypted—across the Internet. The origin and authenticity of the file received may be checked by digital signatures or by MD5 or other message digests. These simple features of the Internet, over a worldwide basis, are changing the basis for the production, sale, and distribution of anything that can be reduced to a computer file for transmission. This includes all manner of office documents, publications, software products, music, photography, video, animations, graphics and the other arts. This in turn is causing seismic shifts in each of the existing industry associations, such as the RIAA and MPAA in the United States, that previously controlled the production and distribution of these products in that country.

Streaming Media

Many existing radio and television broadcasters provide Internet 'feeds' of their live audio and video streams (for example, the BBC). They may also allow time-shift viewing or listening such as Preview, Classic Clips and Listen Again features. These providers have been joined by a range of pure Internet 'broadcasters' who never had on-air licenses. This means that an Internet-connected device, such as a computer or something more specific, can be used to access on-line media in much the same way as was previously possible only with a television or radio receiver. The range of material is much wider, from pornography to highly specialized technical Web-casts. Podcasting is a variation on this theme, where—usually audio—material is first downloaded in full and then may be played back on a computer or shifted to a digital audio player to be listened to on the move. These techniques using simple equipment allow anybody, with little censorship or licensing control, to broadcast audio-visual material on a worldwide basis. Webcams can be seen as an even lower-budget extension of this phenomenon. While some webcams can give full frame rate video, the picture is usually either small or updates slowly. Internet users can watch animals around an African waterhole, ships in the Panama Canal, the traffic at a local roundabout or their own premises, live and in real time. Video chat rooms, video conferencing, and remote controllable webcams are also popular. Many uses can be found for personal webcams in and around the home, with and without two-way sound.

Voice Telephony (VoIP)

VoIP stands for Voice over IP, where IP refers to the Internet Protocol that underlies all Internet communication. This phenomenon began as an optional two-way voice extension to some of the Instant Messaging systems that took off around the year 2000. In recent years many VoIP systems have become as easy to use and as convenient as a normal telephone. The benefit is that, as the Internet carries the actual voice traffic, VoIP can be free or cost much less than a normal telephone call, especially over long distances and especially for those with always-on ADSL or DSL Internet connections.

Thus VoIP is maturing into a viable alternative to traditional telephones. Interoperability between different providers has improved and the ability to call or receive a call from a traditional telephone is available. Simple inexpensive VoIP modems are now available that eliminate the need for a PC.

Voice quality can still vary from call to call but is often equal to and can even exceed that of traditional calls. Remaining problems for VoIP include emergency telephone number dialing and reliability. Currently a few VoIP providers provide some 911 dialing but it is not universally available. Traditional phones are line powered and operate during a power failure, VoIP does not do so without a backup power source for the electronics.

Most VoIP providers offer unlimited national calling but the direction in VoIP is clearly toward global coverage with unlimited minutes for a low monthly fee.

VoIP has also become increasingly popular within the gaming world, as a form of communication between players. Popular gaming VoIP clients include Ventrilo and Teamspeak, and there are others available also.

Censorship

Some governments, such as those of Iran, the People's Republic of China and Cuba, restrict what people in their countries can access on the Internet, especially political and religious content. This is accomplished through software that filters domains and content so that they may not be easily accessed or obtained without elaborate circumvention.

In Norway, Finland and Sweden, major Internet service providers have voluntarily (possibly to avoid such an arrangement being turned into law) agreed to restrict access to sites listed by police. While this list of forbidden URLs is only supposed to contain addresses of known child pornography sites, the content of the list is secret.

Many countries have enacted laws making the possession or distribution of certain material, such as child pornography, illegal, but do not use filtering software.

There are many free and commercially available software programs with which a user can choose to block offensive Web sites on individual computers or networks, such as to limit a child's access to pornography or violence.

Internet Access

Common methods of home access include dial-up, landline broadband (over coaxial cable, fibre optic or copper wires), Wi-Fi, satellite and technology 3G (EVDO) cell phones.

Public places to use the Internet include libraries and Internet cafes, where computers with Internet connections are available. There are also Internet access points in many public places such as airport halls and coffee shops, in some cases just for brief use while standing. Various terms are used, such as "public Internet kiosk", "public access terminal", and "Web payphone". Many hotels now also have public terminals, though these are usually fee-based.

Wi-Fi provides wireless access to computer networks, and therefore can do so to the Internet itself. Hotspots providing such access include Wi-Fi-cafes, where a would-be user needs to bring their own wireless-enabled devices such as a laptop or PDA. These services may be free to all, free to customers only, or fee-based. A hotspot need not be limited to a confined location. The whole campus or park, or even the entire city can be enabled. Grassroots efforts have led to wireless community networks. Commercial WiFi services covering large city areas are in place in London, Vienna, Toronto, San Francisco, Philadelphia, Chicago and Pittsburgh. The Internet can then be accessed from such places as a park bench.

Apart from Wi-Fi, there have been experiments with proprietary mobile wireless networks like Ricochet, various high-speed data services over cellular phone networks, and fixed wireless services.

High-end mobile phones such as smartphones generally come with Internet access through the phone network. Web browsers such as Opera are available on these advanced handsets, which can also run a wide variety of other Internet software. More mobile phones have Internet access than PCs, though this is not as widely used. An Internet access provider and protocol matrix differentiates the methods used to get online.

Leisure

The Internet has been a major source of leisure since before the World Wide Web, with entertaining social experiments such as MUDs and MOOs being conducted on university servers, and humor-related Usenet groups receiving much of the main traffic. Today, many Internet forums have sections devoted to games and funny videos; short cartoons in the form of Flash movies are also popular. Over 6 million people use blogs or message boards as a means of communication and for the sharing of ideas. The pornography and gambling industries have both taken full advantage of the World Wide Web, and often provide a significant source of advertising revenue for other Web sites. Although many governments have attempted to put restrictions on both industries' use of the Internet, this has generally failed to stop their widespread popularity.

A song in the Broadway musical show *Avenue Q* is titled "The Internet is for Porn" and refers to the popularity of this aspect of the Internet. One main area of leisure on the Internet is multiplayer gaming. This form of leisure creates communities, bringing people of all ages and origins to enjoy the fast-paced world of multiplayer games. These range from MMORPG to first-person shooters, from role-playing games to online gambling. This has revolutionized the way many people interact and spend their free time on the Internet. While online gaming has been around since the 1970s, modern modes of online gaming began with services such as GameSpy and MPlayer, which players of games would typically subscribe to. Non-subscribers were limited to certain types of gameplay or certain games. Many use the Internet to access and download music, movies and other works for their enjoyment and relaxation. As discussed above, there are paid and unpaid sources for all of these, using centralized servers and distributed peer-to-peer technologies.

Discretion is needed as some of these sources take more care over the original artists' rights and over copyright laws than others. Many use the World Wide Web to access news, weather and sports reports, to plan and book holidays and to find out more about their random ideas and casual interests.

People use chat, messaging and email to make and stay in touch with friends worldwide, sometimes in the same way as some previously had pen pals. Social networking Web sites like Friends Reunited and many others like them also put and keep people in contact for their enjoyment. The Internet has seen a growing amount of Internet operating systems, where users can access their files, folders, and settings via the Internet. An example of an opensource webos is Eyeos.

Cyberslacking has become a serious drain on corporate resources; the average UK employee spends 57 minutes a day surfing the Web at work, according to a study by Peninsula Business Services

Complex Architecture

Many computer scientists see the Internet as a "prime example of a large-scale, highly engineered, yet highly complex system". The Internet is extremely heterogeneous. (For instance, data transfer rates and physical characteristics of connections vary widely.)

The Internet exhibits "emergent phenomena" that depend on its large-scale organization. For example, data transfer rates exhibit temporal self-similarity. Further adding to the complexity of the Internet is the ability of more than one computer to use the Internet through only one node, thus creating the possibility for a very deep and hierarchal based sub-network that can theoretically be extended infinitely (disregarding the programmatic limitations of the IPv4 protocol).

However, since principles of this architecture date back to the 1960s, it might not be a solution best suited to modern needs, and thus the possibility of developing alternative structures is currently being looked into.

Marketing

The Internet has also become a large market for companies; some of the biggest companies today have grown by taking advantage of the efficient nature of low-cost advertising and commerce through the Internet; also known as e-commerce. It is the fastest way to spread information to a vast amount of people simultaneously. The Internet has also subsequently revolutionized shopping—for example; a person can order a CD online and receive it in the mail within a couple of days, or download it directly in some cases. The Internet has also greatly facilitated personalized marketing which allows a company to market a product to a specific person or a specific group of people more so than any other advertising medium. Examples of personalized marketing include online communities such as MySpace, Friendster, Orkut, and others which thousands of Internet users join to advertise themselves and make friends online.

Many of these users are young teens and adolescents ranging from 13 to 25 years old. In turn, when they advertise themselves they advertise interests and hobbies, which online marketing companies can use as information as to what those users will purchase online, and advertise their own companies' products to those users. A very ineffective way of advertising on the Internet is through spamming an email with advertisements. This is ineffective because, now, most email providers offer protection against email spam. Most spam messages are sent automatically to everybody in the email database of the company/person that is spamming. This way of advertising is almost like using adware.

Internet Today

Aside from the complex physical connections that make up its infrastructure, the Internet is facilitated by bi- or multi-lateral commercial contracts (e.g., peering agreements), and by technical specifications or protocols that describe how to exchange data over the network. Indeed, the Internet is essentially defined by its interconnections and routing policies.

As of March 10, 2007, 1.114 billion people use the Internet according to Internet World Stats.

Internet Protocols

In this context, there are three layers of protocols:

- At the lowest level is IP (Internet Protocol), which defines the datagrams or packets that carry blocks of data from one node to another. The vast majority of today's Internet uses version four of the IP protocol (i.e. IPv4), and although IPv6 is standardized, it exists only as "islands" of connectivity, and there are many ISPs without any IPv6 connectivity.

- Next came TCP (Transmission Control Protocol), UDP (User Datagram Protocol), and ICMP (Internet Control Message Protocol)—the protocols by which data is transmitted. TCP makes a virtual 'connection', which gives some level of guarantee of reliability. UDP is a best-effort, connectionless transport, in which data packets that are lost in transit will not be re-sent. ICMP is connectionless, it is used for control and signaling purposes.
- On top comes the application protocols. This defines the specific messages and data formats sent and understood by the applications running at each end of the communication.

Internet Structure

There have been many analyses of the Internet and its structure. For example, it has been determined that the Internet IP routing structure and hypertext links of the World Wide Web are examples of scale-free networks. Similar to the way the commercial Internet providers connect via Internet exchange points, research networks tend to interconnect into large subnetworks such as:

- GEANT
- GLORIAD
- Abilene Network
- JANET (the UK's Joint Academic Network aka UKERNA)

These in turn are built around relatively smaller networks.

In network schematic diagrams, the Internet is often represented by a cloud symbol, into and out of which network communications can pass.

ICANN

The Internet Corporation for Assigned Names and Numbers (ICANN) is the authority that coordinates the assignment of unique identifiers on the Internet, including domain names, Internet Protocol (IP) addresses, and protocol port and parameter numbers. A globally unified namespace (i.e., a system of names in which there is one and only one holder of each name) is essential for the Internet to function. ICANN is headquartered in Marina del Rey, California, but is overseen by an international board of directors drawn from across the Internet technical, business, academic, and non-commercial communities. The US government continues to have the primary role in approving changes to the root zone file that lies at the heart of the domain name system. Because the Internet is a distributed network comprising many voluntarily interconnected networks, the Internet, as such, has no governing body. ICANN's role in coordinating the assignment of unique identifiers distinguishes it as perhaps the only central coordinating body on the global Internet, but the scope of its authority extends only to the Internet's systems of domain names, IP addresses, and protocol port and parameter numbers.

On November 16, 2005, the World Summit on the Information Society, held in Tunis, established the Internet Governance Forum (IGF) to discuss Internet-related issues.

Language

The prevalent language for communication on the Internet is English. This may be a result of the Internet's origins, as well as English's role as the lingua franca. It may also be related to the poor capability of early computers to handle characters other than those in the basic Latin alphabet.

After English (30% of Web visitors) the most-requested languages on the World Wide Web are Chinese 14%, Japanese 8%, Spanish 8%, German 5%, French 5%, Portuguese 3.5%, Korean 3%, Italian 3% and Arabic 2.5% (from Internet World Stats, updated January 11, 2007). By continent, 36% of the world's Internet users are based in Asia, 29% in Europe, and 21% in North America. The Internet's technologies have developed enough in recent years that good facilities are available for development and communication in most widely used languages. However, some glitches such as *mojibake*.

Internet and the Workplace

The Internet is allowing greater flexibility in working hours and location, especially with the spread of unmetered high-speed connections and Web applications.

The Mobile Internet

The Internet can now be accessed virtually anywhere by numerous means. Mobile phones, datacards, handheld game consoles and cellular routers allow users to connect to the Internet from anywhere there is a cellular network supporting that device's technology.

9

Miscellaneous Issues

"Do not bite at the bait of pleasure till you know there is no hook beneath it."

—Thomas Jefferson

We have described various issues pertaining to mass media and modern forms of it in preceding chapters. Here we will describe some more issues which every media person should be acquainted with.

I

MEDIA CONSOLIDATION

Variously known as 'concentration of media' ownership media consolidation is a commonly used term that refers to the majority of the media outlets being owned by a small number of conglomerates and corporations — especially by those who view such consolidation as detrimental, dangerous, or otherwise problematic — to characterize ownership structure of mass media industries. These individual media industries are often referred to as a 'Media Institution'. Media ownership may refer to states of oligopoly or monopoly in a given media industry, or to the importance of a low number of media conglomerates. Large media conglomerates include Disney, National Amusements, Time Warner, Viacom, News Corp, Bertelsmann AG, Sony, General Electric, Vivendi SA, Hearst Corporation, and Lagardère Group.

For example, movie production is known to be dominated by major studios since the early 20th Century; before that, there was a period in which Edison's Trust monopolised the industry. The music and television industries recently witnessed cases of media consolidation, with Sony Music Entertainment's parent company merging their music division with Bertelsmann AG's BMG to form Sony BMG and TimeWarner's The WB and CBS Corp.'s UPN merging to form The CW. In the case of Sony BMG, there existed a "Big Five" (now "Big Four") of major record companies, while The CW's creation was an attempt to consolidate ratings and stand up to the "Big Four" of American network (terrestrial) television.

There may also be some large-scale owners in an industry that are not the causes of monopoly or oligopoly. Clear Channel Communications, especially since the Telecommunications Act of 1996, acquired many radio stations across the United States, and came to own more than 1,200 stations. However, the radio broadcasting industry in the United States and elsewhere can be regarded as oligopolistic regardless of the existence of such a player. Because radio stations are local in reach, each licensed a specific part of airwave by the FCC in a specific local area, any local market is served by a limited number of stations. In most countries, this system of licensing makes many markets local oligopolies. The similar market structure exists for television broadcasting, cable systems and newspaper industries, all of which are characterised by the existence of large-scale owners. Concentration of ownership is often found in these industries. In the United States, data on ownership and market share of media companies is not held in the public domain. Academics, for example at MIT Media Lab and NYU, have struggled to find data that show reliably the concentration of media ownership.

Concentration of media ownership is very frequently seen as a problem of contemporary media and society. When media ownership is concentrated in one or more of the ways mentioned above, a number of undesirable consequences follow, including the following:

(a) Commercially driven, ultra-powerful mass market media is primarily loyal to sponsors, i.e. advertisers and government rather than to the public interest.

(b) For the general public, there are less diverse opinions and voices available in the media.

(c) If only a few companies representing the interests of a minority elite control the public airwaves of 300 million US citizens, then calling them "public airwaves" is only lip service.

(d) For minorities and others, fewer opportunities are available for voicing their concerns and reaching the public.

(e) Healthy, market-based competition is absent, leading to slower innovation and increased prices.

It is important to elaborate upon the issue of media consolidation and its effect upon the diversity of information reaching a particular market. Critics of consolidation raise the issue of whether monopolistic or oligopolistic control of a local media market can be fully accountable and dependable in serving the public interest. If, for example, only one or two media conglomerates dominate in a single market, the question is not only that of whether they will present a diversity of opinions, but also of whether they are willing to present information that may be damaging to either their advertisers or to themselves.

If it is in the best interests of the media conglomerates

not to run a story or allow a particular opinion, but in the best interests of the public interest to run it, it arguably makes better business sense to opt for the former over the latter. On the local end, reporters have often seen their stories refused or edited beyond recognition, in instances where they have unearthed potentially damaging information concerning either the media outlet's advertisers or its parent company. For example, in 1997, the Fox Broadcasting Company O&O in Tampa, Florida fired two reporters and suppressed a story they had produced about one of the Fox network's major advertisers, Monsanto, concerning the health effects of Bovine Growth Hormone (BGH). Monsanto took action after Fox and threatened to sue over the story.

Another example would be the repeated refusal of networks to air "ads" from anti-war advocates to liberal groups like MoveOn.org, or religious groups like the United Church of Christ, regardless of factual basis. A recent famous case was Super Bowl XXXVIII wherein CBS refused to air an ad criticizing the growing federal budget deficit but aired a spot celebrating the Office of National Drug Control Policy.

Consequently, if the companies dominating a media market choose to suppress stories that do not serve their interests, the public suffers, since they are not adequately informed of some crucial issues that may affect them. If the only media outlets in town refuse to air a story, then the question becomes, who will?

Concern among academia rests in the notion that the purpose of the first amendment to the US constitution was to encourage a free press as political agitator evidenced by the famous quote from US President Thomas Jefferson, "The only security of all is in a free press. The force of public opinion cannot be resisted when permitted freely to be expressed. The agitation it produces must be submitted to. It is necessary, to keep the waters pure." Critics of media deregulation and the resulting concentration of ownership fear that such trends will only continue to reduce the diversity of information provided, as well as to reduce the accountability of information providers to the public. The ultimate consequence of consolidation, critics argue, is a poorly-informed public, restricted to a reduced array of media options that offer only information that does not harm the media oligopoly's growing range of interests.

For those critics, media deregulation is a dangerous trend, facilitating an increase in concentration of media ownership, and subsequently reducing the overall quality and diversity of information communicated through major media channels. Increased concentration of media ownership can lead to the censorship of a wide range of critical thought.

Another concern is that consolidated media is not flexible enough to serve local communities in case of emergency. This happened in Minot, North Dakota, in 2002, after a train filled with anhydrous ammonia derailed. None of the leading radio stations in Minot carried information on the derailment or evacuation procedures, largely because they were all owned by Clear Channel Communications and received automated feeds from the corporate headquarters in San Antonio, Texas. 1600 people were injured and one died. Some typical counter-arguments to the criticisms above include the following:

(a) Reduced cost of operations as a result of consolidation of some functions

(b) Increased competitiveness due to the larger capital of the owners, especially to compete against some of the global, giant media conglomerates

(c) More segmented or differentiated products and services to respond to a wider variety of demands better.

On the other hand, a massive diversification of media, thanks to the Internet, materialised by millions of websites, forums, blogs and wikis is taking place. That evolution, often labeled citizen journalism or citizen media, makes it possible for practically everybody to be a media creator, owner and actor, instead of a passive user.

Citizen media gradually take audiences out of the traditional media and weaken the role of information professionals. Traditional media are slowly trying to adapt by becoming more "participative", asking their readers or watchers to send their own news. Citizen media cannot however function with the same kind of in depth reporting that brick-and-mortar organisations have, in the form of funded research and expert analysis.

Nor is the internet immune to media consolidation. The largest telephone and cable companies which own the infrastructure of the internet have been accused of attempting to control the speed in which users can access various websites. The debate surrounding the independence and public control of the internet is called "net neutrality".

Media Consolidation in Particular Countries

Australia

Controls over media ownership in Australia are laid down in the *Broadcasting Services Act 1992*, administered by the Australian Communications and Media Authority (ACMA). Even with laws in place Australia has a high concentration of media ownership. Ownership of national and the newspapers of each capital city are dominated by two corporations, Rupert Murdoch's News Corporation, (which was founded in Adelaide) and John Fairfax Holdings.These two corporations along with West Australian Newspapers and the Harris Group work together to create Australian Associated Press which distributes the news and then sells it on to other outlets such as the Australian Broadcasting Corporation. Although much of the everyday main stream news is drawn from the Australian Associated Press all the privately owned media outlets still compete with each other for exclusive Pop culture news.

Rural and regional media is dominated by Rural Press Limited which is owned also by John Fairfax Holdings, with significant holdings in all states and territories. Daily Mail and General Trust operate the DMG Radio Australia commercial radic networks in metropolitan and regional areas of Australia. Formed in 1996, it has since become one of the largest radio media companies in the country. The company currently own more than 60 radio stations across New South Wales, Victoria, South Australia, Queensland and Western Australia.

There are rules governing foreign ownership of Australian media and these rules were being considered for loosening by the former Howard Government.

According to Reporters Without Borders in 2004, Australia is in 41st position on a list of countries ranked by Press Freedom; well behind New Zealand (9th) and United Kingdom (28th). This ranking is primarily due to the limited diversity in media ownership. The problem has even created a show in it self *Media Watch* on a government funded station Australian Broadcasting Corporation (ABC) which is one of two government administered free to air channels the other being Special Broadcasting Service (SBS).

Canada

Radio and television ownership in Canada is governed by the CRTC. The CRTC does not regulate ownership of newspapers or Internet media, although ownership in those media may be taken into consideration in decisions pertaining to a licensee's broadcasting operations.

Apart from the public Canadian Broadcasting Corporation and community broadcasters, media in Canada are primarily owned by a small number of companies, including CTVglobemedia, Canwest Global, Rogers, Shaw, Astral, Newcap and Quebecor. Each of these companies holds a diverse mix of television, cable television, radio, newspaper, magazine and/or internet operations. Some smaller media companies also exist. In 2007, CTVglobemedia, Astral Media, Quebecor, Canwest Global and Rogers all expanded significantly, through the acquisitions of CHUM Limited, Standard Broadcasting, Osprey Media, Alliance Atlantis and Citytv, respectively.

Due to Canada's smaller population, some types of media consolidation have always been allowed. In small markets where the population could not adequately support multiple television stations competing for advertising revenue, the CRTC began permitting twinstick operations, in which the same company operated both CBC and CTV affiliates in the same market, in 1967. This model of television ownership was restricted to smaller markets until the mid-1990s, when the CRTC began to allow companies to own multiple television stations in large markets such as Toronto, Montreal and Vancouver.

As of 2007, almost all Canadian television stations are owned by national media conglomerates. Most, in fact, are directly owned and operated by their associated networks, although even private affiliate stations are mostly owned by non-network conglomerates rather than local companies. These acquisitions have been controversial; stations in smaller markets have frequently had their local news programming cut back or even eliminated. For instance, CTV's stations in Northern Ontario and in Atlantic Canada are served by a single regional newscast for each region, with only brief local news inserts for headlines of purely local interest. This, in turn, has contributed to the rise of independent local webmedia such as *SooToday.com*, *The Tyee* and *rabble.ca*.

Many, though not all, Canadian newspapers are also owned by the same media conglomerates which own the television networks. Companies which own both television and newspaper assets have strict controls on the extent to which they can merge the operations. The issue of newspaper ownership has been particularly controversial in Canada, especially in the mid-1990s when Conrad Black's Hollinger acquired the Southam chain. Black's 1999 sale of the Hollinger papers resulted in an increase in the diversity of newspaper ownership, with new ownership groups such as Osprey Media entering the business, but was even more controversial because the CRTC, waiving its former rules against broadcasting companies acquiring newspaper assets, permitted Canwest Global to purchase many of the Hollinger papers. The *Toronto Star* is a partial exception to this — it is owned by an independent company, but is itself a part *owner* of CTVglobemedia.

In radio, a company is normally restricted to owning no more than three stations in a single market, of which only two can be on the same broadcast band. (That is, a company may own two FM stations and an AM station, or two AMs and one FM, but may not own three FMs.) Under certain circumstances, local marketing agreements may be implemented, or the ownership rule may be waived entirely. For example, in Windsor, Ontario, CTVglobemedia owns all of the city's commercial broadcast outlets, due to the city's unique circumstances — being in the immediate environs of the Metro Detroit market in the United States, Windsor has historically been a difficult market for commercial broadcasters, so the CRTC waived its usual ownership restrictions to help protect the Windsor stations' financial viability. When licensing a new broadcast outlet, the CRTC has a general (but not strict) tendency to favour new and local broadcasters. However, in the modern media context such broadcasters often struggle for financial viability, and are often subsequently acquired by larger companies. The CRTC rarely denies the acquisition applications. Canada also has strict laws around non-Canadian ownership of cultural industries; a media company in Canada may not be more than 20 per cent foreign-owned.

Under new rules announced in 2008, the CRTC limited companies to two types of media in a given market — a company may, for example, own television and radio assets in one city, or radio and newspaper, or television and newspaper, but may not own all three simultaneously. As well, with the ownership of cable specialty channels increasingly consolidating under the same few media conglomerates that own most of the country's conventional television stations, the CRTC also imposed a market share cap: no company can own broadcasting assets holding more than 45 per cent of the country's total television viewership.

Europe

United Kingdom

In Britain and Ireland, Rupert Murdoch owns best-selling tabloids News of the World, The Sun as well as the broadsheet The Times and Sunday Times, and satellite broadcasting network BSkyB. Daily Mail and General Trust (DMGT) own The Daily Mail and The Mail on Sunday, The Evening Standard, Ireland on Sunday, and free London daily Metro, and control a large proportion of regional media, including through subsidiary Northcliffe Media, in addition to large shares in ITN and GCap Media.

Republic of Ireland

Independent News & Media (CEO: Tony O'Reilly) owns many national newspapers: the *Evening Herald, Irish Independent, Sunday Independent, Sunday World* and *Irish Daily Star*. It also owns 29.9% of the *Sunday Tribune*.

Germany

Axel Springer AG is one of the largest newspaper publishing companies in Europe, claiming to have over 150 newspapers and magazines in over 30 countries in Europe. In the 1960s and 1970s the company's media followed an aggressive conservative policy (see Springerpresse). It publishes Germany's only nationwide tabloid, Bild and one of Germany's most important broadsheets, Die Welt. Axel Springer also ownes a number on regional newspapers, especially in Saxony and in the Hamburg Metropolitan Region, giving the company a de-facto monopole in the latter case. An attempt to buy one of Germany's two major private TV Groups, ProSiebenSat.1 in 2006 was withdrawn due to large concerns by regulation authorities as well as by parts of the public. The company is also active in Hungary, where it is the biggest publisher of regional newspapers, and in Poland, where it ownes the best-selling tabloid Fakt, one of the nation's most important broadsheets, Dziennik, and is one of the biggest shareholder in #2 private TV company, Polsat.

Bertelsmann is one of the world's largest media companies. It ownes RTL Group, which is one of the two mayor private TV companies in both Germany and the Netherlands and also owning assets in Belgium, France, UK, Spain, Czech and Hungary. Bertelsmann also ownes Gruner+Jahr, Germany's biggest popular magazine publisher, including popular news magazine Stern and a 26% share in investigative news magazine Der Spiegel. Bertelsmann also ownes Random House, a book publisher, #1 in the English-speaking world and #2 in Germany.

Italy

Silvio Berlusconi, the Prime Minister of Italy, is the major shareholder of - by far - Italy's biggest private TV company, Mediaset, Italy's biggest magazine publisher, Mondadori, and Italy's biggest advertising company Publitalia. One of Italy's nationwide dailies, Il Giornale, is owned by his brother. Berlusconi has often been criticised for using the media assets he owns to advance his political career.

United States

Prior to 1927, public airwaves in the United States were regulated by the United States Department of Commerce and largely litigated in the courts as the growing number of stations fought for space in the burgeoning industry. The Federal Radio Act of 1927 (signed into law February 23, 1927) nationalised the airwaves and formed the Federal Radio Commission (later named the Federal Communications Commission, or FCC) to assume control of the airwaves.

The Communications Act of 1934 refined and expanded on the authority of the FCC to regulate public airwaves in the United States, combining and reorganizing provisions from the Federal Radio Act of 1927 and the Mann-Elkins

Act of 1910. It empowered the FCC, among other things, to administer broadcasting licenses, impose penalties and regulate standards and equipment used on the airwaves. The Act also mandated that the FCC would act in the interest of the "public convenience, interest, or necessity." The Act established a system whereby the FCC grants licenses to the spectrum to broadcasters for commercial use, so long as the broadcasters act in the public interest by providing news programming.

Lobbyists from the largest radio broadcasters, ABC and NBC, successfully petitioned to attach a cost to the license required to broadcast, and were thus able to "price out" many amateur broadcasters that had previously existed. Such was the precedent for much of the following regulatory decisions, which have mostly focused on the percentage of a market deemed allowable to a single company. The Telecommunications Act of 1996 set the modern tone of "deregulation," a relaxing of percentage constrictions that solidified the previous history of privatizing the utility and commodifying the spectrum. The legislation, touted as a step that would foster competition, actually resulted in the subsequent mergers of several large companies, a trend which still continues.

The FCC held one official forum, February 27, 2003, in Richmond, Virginia in response to public pressures to allow for more input on the issue of elimination of media ownership limits. Some complain that more than one forum was needed. On June 2, 2003, FCC, in a 3-2 vote under Chairman Michael Powell, approved new media ownership laws that removed many of the restrictions previously imposed to limit ownership of media within a local area. The changes were not, as is customarily done, made available to the public for a comment period.

- Single-company ownership of media in a given market is now permitted up to 45% (formerly 35%, up from 25% in 1985) of that market.
- Restrictions on newspaper and TV station ownership in the same market were removed.
- All TV channels, magazines, newspapers, cable, and Internet services are now counted, weighted based on people's average tendency to find news on that medium. At the same time, whether a channel *actually contains* news is no longer considered in counting the percentage of a medium owned by one owner.
- Previous requirements for periodic review of license have been changed. Licenses are no longer reviewed for "public-interest" considerations.

The decision by the FCC was overturned by the U.S. Third Circuit Court of Appeals in the decision Prometheus Radio Project v. FCC in June, 2004. The Majority ruled 2-1 against the FCC and ordered the Commission to reconfigure how it justified raising ownership limits. The Supreme Court later turned down an appeal, so the ruling stands.

Cross-Ownership Proceedings

The FCC voted December 18, 2007 to relax media ownership rules, including a statute that forbids a single company to own both a newspaper and a television or radio station in the same city. FCC Chairman Kevin Martin circulated the plan in October 2007. Martin's justification for the rule change is to ensure the viability of America's newspapers and to address issues raised in the 2003 FCC decision that was later struck down by the courts. The FCC held six hearings around the country to receive public input from individuals, broadcasters and corporations.

Because of the lack of discussion during the 2003 proceedings, increased attention as been paid to ensuring that the FCC engages in proper dialogue with the public regarding its current rules change.

FCC Commissioners Deborah Taylor-Tate and Robert McDowell joined Chairman Martin in voting in favour of the rule change. Commissioners Michael Copps and Jonathan Adelstein, both Democrats, opposed the change.

By Corporation

- Disney, "New" Viacom (and its former parent CBS Corporation, the former "Old" Viacom), TimeWarner, News Corporation, Bertelsmann AG, and General Electric together own more than 90% of the media holdings in the United States.
- Among other assets, Disney owns ABC, Buena Vista Motion Pictures Group, ESPN, and Miramax Films.
- CBS Corporation owns CBS, CBS Radio (formerly Infinity Radio), Simon & Schuster editing group, a 50% ownership stake in The CW, etc.
- Time Warner owns CNN, *Time*, AOL, a 50% ownership stake in The CW, etc.
- Bertelsmann owns Arvato, Direct Group, RTL Group (which owns VOX and Five and a part in M6 TV channel), etc.
- Triton Media Group is rapidly consolidating assets in the radio industry, acquiring Dial Global, Waitt Radio Networks and Jones Radio Networks, three major satellite music radio providers.
- Lagardère Group owns Hachette Filipacchi Médias, which is the largest magazine publisher in the world, 100% of Lagardère Media, 34% of CanalSat,

and Hachette Livre (as well as parts in the European military aerospace EADS company).

- Vivendi owns Canal + Group, Universal Music Group and 20% of NBC Universal.
- Edouard de Rothschild has 37% of French left-wing daily *Libération* since 2005.
- Arms company Dassault owns 82% of the *Socpresse*, which controls conservative *Le Figaro* (in which the Carlyle Group previously had a 40% stake), as well as *L'Express*.
- *Le Monde* is owned by *La Vie Le Monde*, which also controls *Télérama* and other publications of *La Vie Catholique*, as well as 51% of *Le Monde diplomatique*.
- French Bouygues company owns 42.9% of TF1 TV channel, and is the parent company of Bouygues Télécom.
- Rupert Murdoch, the media magnate, apart of News Corp., also owns British *News of the World*, *The Sun*, *The Times*, and *The Sunday Times*, as well as the Sky Television network, which merged with British Satellite Broadcasting to form BSkyB, and SKY Italia; in the US, he owns the *Fox Networks* and the *New York Post*. Since 2003, he also owns 34% of DirecTV Group (formerly Hughes Electronics), operator of the largest American satellite TV system, DirecTV, and Intermix Media (creators of myspace.com) since 2005. *See also Murdoch Newspaper List*.
- Modern Times Group, quoted on the Stockholm Stock Exchange, owns Viasat TV network and Metro International, which is the world's largest chain of

free newspapers, publishing 57 daily Metro editions in 18 countries.

- In the UK, Daily Mail and General Trust plc owns newspapers including the Daily Mail, Euromoney Institutional Investor PLC, has a 29.9% stake in GCap Media (the owner of Classic FM and other radio stations), and a 20% stake in ITN, and also own regional publisher Northcliffe Media.
- Bolloré, owned by Vincent Bolloré, who is Havas's main share-holder and president and UK group Aegis' first share-holder. Bolloré owns Direct 8 French TV channel.
- Arnoldo Mondadori Editore control a large share of the magazine publishing industry in Italy.

Film Documentaries

- *Orwell Rolls in His Grave* (2004) documentary available on DVD considers media concentration in the U.S.
- *Beyond Citizen Kane* by Simon Hartog (1993); about Roberto Marinho's Globo Group in Brazil.

[Source: Wikipedia]

II
MEDIA LITERACY

It is remarkable to note that Media education is developing in Great Britain, Australia, South Africa, Canada, the United States, with a growing interest in the Netherlands, Italy, Greece, Austria, Switzerland, India, Russia and among many other countries of the world.

Media literacy is the process of accessing, analyzing, evaluating and creating messages in a wide variety of media modes, genres and forms. It uses an inquiry-based instructional model that encourages people to ask questions about what they watch, see and read. Media literacy education is one means of developing media literacy. It provides tools to help people critically analyze messages to detect propaganda, censorship, and bias in news and public affairs programming (and the reasons for such), and to understand how structural features — such as media ownership, or its funding model — affect the information presented. Media literacy aims to enable people to be skillful creators and producers of media messages, both to facilitate an understanding as to the strengths and limitations of each medium, as well as to create independent media. Media literacy is an expanded conceptualisation of literacy. By transforming the process of media consumption into an active and critical process, people gain greater awareness of the potential for misrepresentation and manipulation (especially through commercials and public relations techniques), and understand the role of mass media and participatory media in constructing views of reality.

Media literacy was originally conceived as an educational tool to protect people from what many perceived to be mass media's ill effects. The earliest country known to use this inoculative paradigm was Great Britain in the 1930s. In the 1960s, there was a paradigm shift in the field of media literacy to emphasize working within popular culture rather than trying to convince people that popular culture was primarily destructive. This was known as the popular arts paradigm. In the 1980s, there came a recognition that the ideological power of the media was tied to the naturalisation of the image. Constructed messages were being passed off as natural ones. The focus of media literacy also shifted to the consumption of images and representations, also known as the representational paradigm. In the United Kingdom and Australia media literacy is often a stand alone credit course, as well as part of the English curricula.

In Australia, media education was influenced by developments in Britain related to the inoculation, popular arts and demystification approaches. Key theorists who influenced Australian media education were Graeme Turner and John Hartley who helped develop Australian media and cultural studies. During the 1980s and 1990s, Western Australians Robyn Quin and Barrie MacMahon wrote seminal text books such as *Real Images*, translating many complex media theories into classroom appropriate learning frameworks. Currently, in most Australian states, media is one of five strands of the Arts Key Learning Area and includes "essential learnings" or "outcomes" listed for various stages of development. At the senior level (years 11 and 12), several states offer Media Studies as an elective. For example, many Queensland schools offer Film, Television and New Media, while Victorian schools offer VCE Media. Media education is supported by the teacher professional association Australian Teachers of Media (ATOM) which publishes a range of resources and the excellent Screen Education. Remarkably, in European countries media education has seen many different forms. Media education was introduced into the Finnish elementary curriculum in 1970 and into high schools in 1977. But the media education we know today did not evolve in Finland until the 1990s. Media education has been compulsory in Sweden since 1980 and in Denmark since 1970. In both Nordic countries, media education evolved in the 1980s and 1990s as media education gradually moved away from moralizing attitudes towards an approach that is more searching and pupil-centred. In 1994, the Danish education bill gave recognition to media education but it is still not an integrated part of the school. The focus in Denmark seems to be on information technology. France has taught film from the inception of the medium, but it has only been recently that conferences and media courses for teachers have been organised with the inclusion of media production. Germany saw theoretical publications on media literacy in the 1970s and 80s, with a growing interest for media education inside and outside the educational system in the 80s and 90s. In the Netherlands media literacy was placed in the agenda by the Dutch government in 2006 as an important subject for the Dutch society.

In April, 2008, an official center has been created (mediawijsheid expertisecentrum = medialiteracy expertisecenter) by the Dutch government. This center is more a network organisation existing out of different partners who have their own expertise with the subject of media education. The idea is that media education will become a part of the official curriculum. The history of Media Education in Russia goes back to the 1920s. The first attempts to instruct in media education (on the press and film materials, with the vigorous emphasis on the communist ideology) appeared in the 1920s but were stopped by Stalin's repressions. The end of the 1950s - the beginning of the 1960s was the time of the revival of media education in secondary schools, universities, after-school children centers (Moscow, Petersburg, Voronezh, Samara, Kurgan, Tver, Rostov, Taganrog, Novosibirsk, Ekaterinburg, etc.), the revival of media education seminars and conferences for the teachers.

During the time when the intensive rethinking of media education approaches was on the upgrade in the Western hemisphere, in Russia of the 1970s–1980s media education was still developing within the aesthetic concept. Among the important achievements of 1970s-1990s one can recall the first official programmes of film and media education, published by Ministry of Education, increasing interest of Ph.D. to media education, experimental theoretic and practical work on media education by O.Baranov (Tver), S.Penzin (Voronezh), G.Polichko, U.Rabinovich (Kurgan), Y.Usov (Moscow), A.Fedorov (Taganrog), A.Sharikov (Moscow) and others. The important events in media education development in Russia are the registration of the new specialisation (since 2002) for the pedagogical universities – 'Media Education' ([1] 03.13.30), and the launch of a new academic journal 'Media Education' (since January 2005), partly sponsored by the ICOS UNESCO 'Information for All'. Additionally, the Internet sites of Russian Association for Film and Media Education (English and Russian versions) were created. Taking into account the fact that UNESCO defines media education as the priority field of the cultural educational development in the XXI century, media literacy has good prospects in Russia.

In North America, the beginnings of a formalised approach to media literacy as a topic of education is often attributed to the 1978 formation of the Ontario Association for Media Literacy (AML). Before that time, instruction in media education was usually the purview of individual teachers and practitioners. Canada is the first country in North America to require media literacy in the school curriculum. Every province has mandated media education in its curriculum. For example, in Quebec the new curriculum mandates media literacy from Grade 1 right up to the final year of secondary school (Secondary V). The launching of media education in Canada came about for two reasons. One reason was the concern about the pervasiveness of American popular culture and the other was the education system-driven necessity of contexts for new educational paradigms. Media education is less widespread in formal schooling in the United States, in part because of the decentralised nature of the education system in a country with 70 million children now in public or private schools. There is no central authority making nationwide curriculum recommendations, and each of the fifty states has numerous school districts, each of which operates with a great degree of independence from one another.

As of 2004, Montana became the first state to develop educational standards around media literacy that students are required to be competent in by grades 4, 8, and 12. Additionally, an increasing number of school districts have begun to develop school-wide programmes, elective courses, and other after-school opportunities for media analysis and production. Nearly all 50 states have language that supports media literacy in state curriculum frameworks. Leading universities such as Appalachian State University, Columbia University, New York University, the University of Texas-Austin, and Temple University offer courses and summer institutes in media literacy for pre-service teachers and graduate students. Brigham Young University offers a graduate programme in media education specifically for inservice teachers.

In South Africa, the increasing demand for Media Education has evolved from the dismantling of apartheid and the 1994 democratic elections. The first national Media Education conference in South Africa was actually held in 1990 and the new national curriculum has been in the writing stages since 1997. Since this curriculum strives to reflect the values and principles of a democratic society there seems to be an opportunity for critical literacy and Media Education in Languages and Culture courses.

III

MEDIA DEMOCRACY

Primarily, Media democracy is a production and distribution model which promotes a mass media system that informs and empowers all members of society, and enhances democratic values. The term also refers to a modern social movement evident in countries all over the world which attempts to make mainstream media more accountable to the publics they serve and to create more democratic alternatives.

It is a concept and a social movement that has grown as a response to the increased corporate domination of mass media and the perceived shrinking of the marketplace of ideas. Its proponents advocate monitoring and reforming the mass media, strengthening public service broadcasting, and developing and participating in alternative media and citizen journalism.

Media democracy is a difficult term to define, since in addition to being a concept, it is also an advocacy movement being advanced by a number of academics and grassroots organisations, each with its own methods and goals.

No doubt, it is also difficult to define because the term democracy itself is contested. Market liberals would claim that democracy is best served by the media if there is a minimalist state that allows for private media ownership, does not censor content, or require public-interest broadcasting. In this way, the market would facilitate technological innovation and provide whatever fare the consumer demands. By contrast, media democracy advocates argue that corporate ownership and commercial pressures influence media content, sharply limiting the range of news, opinions, and entertainment citizens receive. Consequently, they call for a more equal distribution of economic, social, cultural, and information capital, which would lead to a more informed citizenry, as well as a more enlightened, representative political discourse. More radical thinkers argue that media democracy remains an under-defined concept because of deliberate structural pressures that prevent individuals from questioning the connection between media and democracy.

A leading proponent of this view is Noam Chomsky, who argues that. The concept of "democratizing the media" has no real meaning within the terms of political discourse in the United States. In fact, the phrase has a paradoxical or even vaguely subversive ring to it. Citizen participation would be considered an infringement on freedom of the press, a blow struck against the independence of the media that would distort the mission they have undertaken to inform the public without fear or favour... this is because the general public must be reduced to its traditional apathy and obedience, and driven from the arena of political debate and action, if democracy is to survive.

Despite the difficulties in defining the term, the concept broadly encompasses the following notions: that the health of the democratic political system depends on the efficient, accurate, and complete transmission of social, political, and cultural information in society; that the media are the conduits of this information and should act in the public interest; that the mass media have increasingly been unable and uninterested in fulfilling this role due to increased concentration of ownership and commercial pressures; and that this undermines democracy as voters and citizens are unable to participate knowledgably in public policy debates. Without an informed and engaged citizenry, policy issues become defined by political and corporate elites. A related element of this concept examines the lack of representation of a diversity of voices and viewpoints, particularly of those who have traditionally been marginalised by mass media.

Main Theories

A key idea of media democracy is that the concentration of media ownership in recent decades in the hands of a few corporations and conglomerates has led to a narrowing of the range of voices and opinions being expressed in the mass media; to an increase in the commercialisation of news and information; to a hollowing out of the news media's ability to conduct investigative reporting and act as the public watchdog; and to an increase of emphasis on the bottom line, which prioritizes infotainment and celebrity news over informative discourse. This concentration has been encouraged by government deregulation and neo-liberal trade policies. For example, the U.S. Telecommunications Act of 1996 discarded most media ownership rules that were previously in place, leading to massive consolidation in the telecommunications industry. Over 4,000 radio stations were bought out, and minority ownership of TV stations dropped to its lowest point since the federal government began tracking such data in 1990. In its review of the Telecommunication Act in 2003, the Federal Communications Commission (FCC) further reduced restrictions and allowed media corporations to grow and expand into other areas of media. The past decade has also seen a number of media corporate mergers and takeovers in Canada. For example, in 1990, 17.3% of daily newspapers were independently owned; in 2005, 1% were.

These changes, among others, caused the Senate Standing Committee on Transport and Communications to launch a study of Canadian news media in March 2003. (This topic had been examined twice in the past, by the Davey Commission (1970) and the Kent Commission (1981), both of which produced recommendations that were never implemented in any meaningful way.)

The Senate Committee's final report , released in June 2006, expressed concern about the effects of the current levels of news media ownership in Canada. Specifically, the Committee discussed their concerns regarding the following trends: the potential of media ownership concentration to limit news diversity and reduce news quality; the Canadian Radio-television and Telecommunications Commission]] (CRTC) and Competition Bureau's ineffectiveness at stopping media ownership concentration; the lack of federal funding for the CBC and the broadcaster's uncertain mandate and role; diminishing employment standards for journalists (including less job security, less journalistic freedom, and new contractual threats to intellectual property); a lack of Canadian training and research institutes; and difficulties with the federal government's support for print media and the absence of funding for the internet-based news media.

The report provided 40 recommendations and 10 suggestions (for areas outside of federal government jurisdiction), including legislation amendments that would trigger automatic reviews of a proposed media merger if certain thresholds are reached, and CRTC regulation revisions to ensure that access to the broadcasting system is encouraged and that a diversity of news and information programming is available through these services.

Media democracy advocates argue in favour of such legislative policies that encourage a stronger commitment to serving the public interest and a commercial framework that facilitates independent media ownership. The 2004 documentary film *Outfoxed: Rupert Murdoch's War on Journalism* treats criticism about corporate media concentration.

Public broadcasting serves as an important counterweight to commercial media, and as such, it is a key element of media democracy. Since public television and radio broadcasters are usually funded by government and/or individual donations, they are not subject to the same commercial pressures as private broadcasters and are therefore an important source of a more diverse and in-depth media content. However, in many countries, public broadcasters are subject to funding instability, which jeopardizes their ability to fulfill their public service role consistently.

As a response to the shortcomings of the mainstream media, proponents of media democracy often advocate supporting and engaging in independent and alternative media, in both print and electronic forms. Through citizen journalism and citizen media, individuals can produce and disseminate information and opinions that are marginalised by the mainstream media. In the book *We the Media: Grassroots Journalism by the People, for the People*, Dan Gillmor urges individuals who are concerned about media ownership concentration and the decreasing amount of public-interest broadcasting to use technology like the internet to create and distribute information they believe is not properly reported in the mainstream news media. This book details strategies that individuals and groups can use to democratize the media.

Activism

There is a growing grassroots media democracy

movement in western industrialised countries. As well as encouraging people to create and disseminate their own news, this movement encourages individuals to critically examine their media content and demand appropriate reforms. The principles of most Media Democracy organisations can be found in the Bill of Media Rights.

The organisations themselves have been active in lobbying for media reform and fighting further deregulation and consolidation of big media. While they have had limited success in the area of media reform, they have been able to put roadblocks in further consolidation of large media companies. When in June 2003 the Federal Communications Commission removed restrictions that limited ownership of the media within a local area, media advocacy organisations such as the Prometheus Radio Project and Media Alliance were able to successfully challenge the changes in court. The FCC is currently revising its June 2003 decision.

Instance of Wikipedia and Wikinews

Wikipedia has become a powerful media democracy tool. Anyone—regardless of educational background, experience, or in-depth knowledge—can edit, expand, or remove content. Individuals do not have to get the approval of an editorial board to post content. While there are administrators on Wikipedia, they have roughly the same powers as ordinary users. Wikipedia also lacks corporate control: Wikipedia operates as a not-for-profit, and accepts no advertising or corporate investment which can influence or silence particular ideas. Operating costs are paid by typically small individual donations.

However, there are criticisms. While internet access is pervasive throughout North America, there is far less access in many other parts of the world. Those without access obviously cannot benefit from, or add information to, Wikipedia. There is also a concern that Wikipedia's content is biased towards a particular group, since a small number of relatively similar individuals contribute much of Wikipedia's content. To address this concern, a group of Wikipedia users have established Wikipedia:WikiProject Countering systemic bias to create articles and further develop existing articles in neglected subject areas on Wikipedia.

In 2004, Wikimedia established a site called Wikinews dedicated solely to providing news coverage using wiki technology and the open collaborative philosophy. The site's mission statement commits it to, "present up-to-date, relevant, newsworthy and entertaining content without bias" in the spirit of participatory journalism. Wikinews contains synthesis articles, where a number of news sources are condensed into a single article, and original reporting, where individuals write news stories to fill the gaps of the traditional news media due to various systemic constraints, blind spots, and biases of traditional news media sources do not allow. Unfortunately, Wikinews has not received the same public interest as Wikipedia. Consequently, there is a relatively small number of contributors, and some stories are very short. However, the number of contributor accounts and new articles is increasing. In April 2006, the English edition of Wikinews reached 5,000 articles.

IV

MEDIA MANIPULATION

Media manipulation is an aspect of public relations in which partisans create an image or argument that favours their particular interests. Such tactics may include the use of logical fallacies and propaganda techniques, and often involve the suppression of information or points of view by crowding them out, by inducing other people or groups of people to stop listening to certain arguments, or by simply diverting attention elsewhere.

Distraction by Nationalism

This is a variant on the traditional ad hominem and bandwagon fallacies applied to entire countries. The method is to discredit opposing arguments by appealing to nationalistic pride or memory of past accomplishments, or appealing to fear or dislike of a specific country, or of foreigners in general. It can be very powerful as it discredits foreign journalists (the ones that are least easily manipulated by domestic political or corporate interests).

- Example: "You want to know what I really think of the Europeans?" asked the senior United States State Department official. "I think they have been wrong on just about every major international issue for the past 20 years."
- Example: "Your idea sounds similar to what they are proposing in Turkey. Are you saying the Turks have a better country than us?"
- Example: "The only criticisms of this proposed treaty come from the United States. But we all know that Americans are arrogant and uneducated, so their complaints are irrelevant." (Note that sarcasm is often difficult to detect in textual form.) Example: The "Support Our Troops" campaign created by the Republican party during the War on Terror implies that opposing the war effort detracts support away from the individual soldiers fighting the war. Thus patriotic support of the troops becomes a form of support for the war in general.

Distraction by Scapegoat

A combination of straw man and ad hominem, in which your weakest opponent (or easiest to discredit) is considered as your only important opponent. Example: If many countries are opposed to our actions, but one of them (say, France) is obviously acting out of self-interest, mention mostly France. As with most persuasion methods, it can easily be applied in reverse, in this case, attempting to discredit George W. Bush in order to discredit the entire coalition against Iraq.

Straw Man Fallacy

The "straw man fallacy" is the lumping of a strong opposition argument together with one or many weak ones to create a simplistic weak argument that can easily be refuted. Example: Grouping all opposed to the 2003 invasion of Iraq as "pacifists", so they can be refuted by arguments for war in general. As with most persuasion methods, it can easily be applied in reverse, in this case, to group all those who supported the invasion together and label them as "warmongers" or "lackeys of the United States".

Distraction by Semantics

This involves using euphemistically pleasing terms to obscure the truth. For example saying "choice" or "reproductive rights" instead of referring to the medical term "abortion", or, similarly, "pro-life" instead of "anti-abortion". A brilliantly executed example was the way that President Lincoln's Emancipation Proclamation prevented European nations from entering the war in support of the Confederacy by framing the war in terms of the moral issue "slavery" as opposed to states rights.

Distraction by Phenomenon

A risky but effective strategy summarised best, perhaps, by David Mamet's 1997 movie *Wag the Dog*, by which the public can be distracted, for long periods of time, from an important issue, by one which occupies more news time. When the strategy works, you have a war or other media event taking attention away from misbehaving or crooked leaders. When the strategy does not work, the leader's misbehaviour remains in the press, and the war is derided as an attempted distraction.

Appeals to Consensus

By appealing to a real or fictional "consensus" the media manipulator attempts to create the perception that his opinion is the only opinion, so that alternate ideas are dismissed from public consideration. Michael Crichton explains:

Historically, the claim of consensus has been the first refuge of scoundrels; it is a way to avoid debate by claiming that the matter is already settled. Whenever you hear the consensus of scientists agrees on something or other, reach for your wallet, because you're being had.

Let's be clear: the work of science has nothing whatever to do with consensus.

Consensus is the business of politics. Science, on the contrary, requires only one investigator who happens to be right, which means that he or she has results that are verifiable by reference to the real world. In science consensus is irrelevant. What is relevant is reproducible results. The greatest scientists in history are great precisely because they broke with the consensus.

Marginalisation

This is a widespread and subtle form of media manipulation: simply giving credence only to "mainstream" sources of information; it exists in many news outlets. Information, arguments, and objections that come from other sources are simply considered "fringe" and ignored, or their proponents permanently discredited, or accused of having their own agenda. Example: "I think there are a lot of people out there who feel the way I do, but haven't wanted to come forward because they're afraid of being identified with a fringe group..." Langley said. "I don't believe in all the things that all the (anti-war) groups stand for, but we all do share one thing in common: I do believe that this war is wrong."

Example: "Because Mike Gravel has not demonstrated measurable public support for his campaign to date, he has not received an invitation to the 2008 Democratic Presidential Candidate Debates]."

Demonisation of the Opposition

This is a more general case of distraction by nationalism. Opposing views are ascribed to an out-group or hated group, and thus dismissed out of hand. This approach, carried to extremes, becomes a form of suppression, as in McCarthyism, where anyone disapproving of the government was considered "un-American" and "Communist" and was likely to be denounced. Example: The consignment of almost all dissent to the "International Jewish conspiracy" by Nazi Germany.

Googlewashing

This is a new word coined by Andrew Orlowski of *The Register* in April 2003 to describe the alleged practice of changing the meaning of a meme (in this example, Second Superpower) by web-publishing a well-linked article using the term in an inoffensive manner, stripped of its political significance. Google has also been observed to exclude certain sites from the search function (notably Google.fr and or Google.de).

People concerned about media manipulation have promoted the teaching of media literacy to teach about the above techniques and thus make them less effective with people thus educated.

V

FREEDOM OF THE PRESS

Freedom of the press consists of constitutional or statutory protections pertaining to the media and published materials. With respect to governmental information, any government distinguishes which materials are public or protected from disclosure to the public based on classification of information as sensitive, classified or secret and being otherwise protected from disclosure due to relevance of the information to protecting the national interest.

Many governments are also subject to sunshine laws or freedom of information legislation that are used to define the ambit of national interest.

The Universal Declaration of Human Rights states: *"Everyone has the right to freedom of opinion and expression; this right includes freedom to hold opinions without interference, and impart information and ideas through any media regardless of frontiers"*

This philosophy is usually accompanied by legislation ensuring various degrees of freedom of scientific research (known as scientific freedom), publishing, press and printing the depth to which these laws are entrenched in a country's legal system can go as far down as its constitution. The concept of freedom of speech is often covered by the same laws as freedom of the press, thereby giving equal treatment to media and individuals.

Besides legal definitions, some non-governmental organisations use other criteria to judge the level of press freedom around the world:

(a) Reporters Without Borders considers the number of journalists murdered, expelled or harassed, and the existence of a state monopoly on TV and radio, as well as the existence of censorship and self-censorship in the media, and the overall independence of media as well as the difficulties that foreign reporters may face.

(b) The Committee to Protect Journalists (CPJ) uses the tools of journalism to help journalists by tracking press freedom issues through independent research, fact-finding missions, and firsthand contacts in the field, including local working journalists in countries around the world. CPJ shares information on breaking cases with other press freedom organisations worldwide through the International Freedom of Expression Exchange, a global e-mail network. CPJ also tracks journalist deaths and detentions. CPJ staff applies strict criteria for each case; researchers independently investigate and verify the circumstances behind each death or imprisonment.

(c) Freedom House likewise studies the more general political and economic environments of each nation in order to determine whether relationships of dependence exist that limit in practice the level of press freedom that might exist in theory. So the concept of independence of the press is one closely linked with the concept of press freedom.

Worldwide Press Freedom Index

Every year, Reporters Without Borders establishes a ranking of countries in terms of their freedom of the press. The Worldwide press freedom index list is based on responses to surveys sent to journalists that are members of partner organisations of the RWB, as well as related specialists such as researchers, jurists and human rights activists. The survey asks questions about direct attacks on journalists and the media as well as other indirect sources of pressure against the free press, such as pressure on journalists by non-governmental groups. RWB is careful to note that the index only deals with press freedom, and does not measure the quality of journalism.

In 2003, the countries where press was the most free were Finland, Iceland, the Netherlands and Norway. In 2004, apart from the above countries, Denmark, Ireland, Slovakia, Portugal and Switzerland were tied at the top of the list, followed by New Zealand and Latvia.

The country with the least degree of press freedom was North Korea, followed by Burma, Turkmenistan, People's Republic of China (mainland only), Vietnam, Nepal,and Iran.

Non-Democratic States

According to Reporters Without Borders, more than a third of the world's people live in countries where there is no press freedom. Overwhelmingly, these people live in countries where there is no system of democracy or where there are serious deficiencies in the democratic process.

Freedom of the press is an extremely problematic problem/concept for most non-democratic systems of government since, in the modern age, strict control of access to information is critical to the existence of most non-democratic governments and their associated control systems and security apparatus. To this end, most non-democratic societies employ state-run news organisations to promote the propaganda critical to maintaining an existing political power base and suppress (often very brutally, through the use of police, military, or intelligence agencies) any significant attempts by the media or individual journalists to challenge the approved "government line" on contentious issues. In such countries, journalists operating on the fringes of what is deemed to be acceptable will very often find themselves the subject of considerable intimidation by agents of the state. This can range from simple threats to their professional careers (firing, professional blacklisting to death threats, kidnapping, torture, and assassination.

Reporters Without Borders reports that, in 2003, 42 journalists lost their lives pursuing their profession and that, in the same year, at least 130 journalists were in prison as a result of their occupational activities. In 2005, 63 journalists and 5 media assistants were killed worldwide. In Nepal, Eritrea and China (mainland only), journalists may spend years in jail simply for using the "wrong" word or photo. The Georgiy R. Gongadze case in Ukraine (information needed, spammer removed information). According to the Press Freedom Index for 2007, Iran ranked 166th out of 169 nations. Only three other countries - Eritrea, North Korea and Turkmenistan - had more restrictions on news media freedom than Iran. The government of Mahmoud Ahmadinejad and the Supreme National Security Council had imprisoned 50 journalists in 2007 and had all but eliminated press freedom. Reporters

Without Borders (RWB) has dubbed Iran the "Middle East's biggest prison for journalists."

Regions Closed to Foreign Reporters

- Chechnya, Russia
- Jaffna, Sri Lanka
- Myanmar (Burma)
- Papua, Indonesia
- Waziristan, Pakistan
- Gaza Strip, Palestine
- Tibet, People's Republic of China

Sweden

Arguably, the world's first Freedom of the Press Act was introduced in Sweden in 1766.

Denmark-Norway

Between September 4, 1770 and October 7, 1771 the kingdom of Denmark-Norway had the most unrestricted freedom of press of any country in Europe. This occurred during the regime of Johann Friedrich Struensee, whose first act was to abolish the old censorship laws. However, due to the great amount of mostly anonymous pamphlets published that was critical and often slanderous towards Struensees own regime, he reinstated some restrictions regarding the freedom of press a year later, October 7 1771.

England

The Glorious Revolution of 1688 in England established parliamentary sovereignty over the Crown and, above all, the right of revolution. A major contributor to Western liberal theory was John Locke. Locke argued in *Two Treatises of Government* that the individual placed some of his rights present in the state of nature in trusteeship with the sovereign (government) in return for protection of certain natural individual rights. A social contract was entered into by the people.

Until 1694, England had an elaborate system of licensing. No publication was allowed without the accompaniment of a government-granted license. Fifty years earlier, at a time of civil war, John Milton wrote his pamphlet *Areopagitica*. In this work Milton argued forcefully against this form of government censorship and parodied the idea, writing "when as debtors and delinquents may walk abroad without a keeper, but unoffensive books must not stir forth without a visible jailer in their title." Although at the time it did little to halt the practice of licensing it would be viewed later a significant milestone in press freedom.

Milton's central argument was that the individual is capable of using reason and distinguishing right from wrong, good from bad. In order to be able to exercise this ration right, the individual must have unlimited access to the ideas of his fellow men in "a free and open encounter." From Milton's writings developed the concept of the open marketplace of ideas, the idea that when people argue against each other, the good arguments will prevail. One form of speech that was widely restricted in England was seditious libel, and laws were in place that made criticizing the government a crime. The King was above public criticism and statements critical of the government were forbidden, according to the English Court of the Star Chamber. Truth was not a defense to seditious libel because the goal was to prevent and punish all condemnation of the government.

John Stuart Mill approached the problem of authority versus liberty from the viewpoint of a 19th century utilitarian:

The individual has the right of expressing himself so long as he does not harm other individuals. The good society is one in which the greatest number of persons enjoy the greatest possible amount of happiness. Applying these general principles of liberty to freedom of expression, Mill states that if we silence an opinion, we may silence the truth. The individual freedom of expression is therefore essential to the well-being of society.

Mill's application of the general principles of liberty is expressed in his book On Liberty: "If all mankind minus one, were of one opinion, and one, and only one person were of the contrary opinion, mankind would be no more justified in silencing that one person, than he, if he had the power, would be justified in silencing mankind".

Nazi Germany

The dictatorship of Adolf Hitler largely suppressed freedom of the press through Joseph Goebbels' Ministry of Public Enlightenment and Propaganda. As the Ministry's name implies, propaganda did not carry the negative connotations that it does today (or did in the Allied countries); how-to manuals were openly distributed by that same ministry explaining the craft of effective propaganda. The Ministry also acted as a central control-point for all media, issuing orders as to what stories could be run and what stories would be suppressed. Anyone involved in the film industry — from directors to the lowliest assistant — had to sign an oath of loyalty to the Nazi Party, due to opinion-changing power Goebbels perceived movies to have. (Goebbels himself maintained some personal control over every single film made in Nazi Europe.) Journalists who crossed the Propaganda Ministry were routinely imprisoned or shot as traitors.

India

The Indian Constitution, while not mentioning the word "press", provides for *"the right to freedom of speech and expression"* (Article 19(1) a). However this right is subject to restrictions under sub clause (2), whereby this freedom can be restricted for reasons of "sovereignty and integrity of India, the security of the State, friendly relations with foreign States, public order, preserving decency, preserving morality, in relation to contempt, court, defamation, or incitement to an offense". Laws such as the Official Secrets Act and Prevention of Terrorism Act (PoTA) have been used to limit press freedom. Under PoTA, person could be detained for up to six months for being in contact with a terrorist or terrorist group. PoTA was repealed in 2006, but the Official Secrets Act 1923 continues.

For the first half-century of independence, media control by the state was the major constraint on press freedom. Indira Gandhi famously stated in 1975 that All India Radio is "a Government organ, it is going to remain a Government organ..." With the liberalisation starting in the 1990s, private control of media has burgeoned, leading to increasing independence and greater scrutiny of government. Organisations like Tehelka and NDTV have been particularly influential, e.g. in bringing about the resignation of powerful Haryana minister Venod Sharma.however this freedom of speech and expression is automatically canceled during emergency.the word Reasonable was not present in the original article 19(1)(a. but this was later on added to this article. and presently in India there are number of organisation who are really influential.

Implications of New Technologies

Many of the traditional means of delivering information are being slowly superseded by the increasing pace of modern technological advance. Almost every conventional mode of media and information dissemination has a modern counterpart that offers significant potential advantages to journalists seeking to maintain and enhance their 'freedom of speech'. A few simple examples of such phenomena include:

(a) Terrestrial television versus satellite television: Whilst terrestrial television is relatively easy to manage and manipulate, satellite television is much more difficult to control as journalistic content can easily be broadcast from other jurisdictions beyond the control of individual governments. An example of this in the Middle East is the satellite broadcaster Al Jazeera. This Arabic language media channel operates out of the 'relatively liberal' state of Qatar, and often presents views and content that are problematic to a number of governments in the region and beyond. However, because of the increased affordability and miniaturisation of satellite technology (e.g. dishes and receivers) it is simply not practicable for most states to control popular access to the channel.

(b) Voice over Internet protocol (VOIP) vs. conventional telephony: Although conventional telephony systems are easily tapped and recorded, modern VOIP technology can employ sophisticated encryption systems to evade central monitoring systems. As VOIP and similar technologies become more widespread they are likely to make the effective monitoring of journalists (and their contacts and activities) a very difficult task for governments.

(c)Web-based publishing (e.g., blogging) vs. traditional publishing: Traditional magazines and newspapers rely on physical resources (e.g. offices, printing presses) that can easily be targeted and forced to close down. Web-based publishing systems can be run using ubiquitous and inexpensive equipment and can operate from any global jurisdiction. To get control over web publications, nations and organisations are using Geolocation and Geolocation software.

Gradually, governments are responding to the challenges posed by new media technologies by deploying increasingly sophisticated technology of their own (a notable example being China's attempts to impose control through a state run internet service provider that controls access to the Internet) but it seems that this will becomes an ever increasingly difficult task as journalists continue to find new ways to exploit technology and stay one step ahead of the generally slower moving government institutions that attempt to censor them.

Organisations for Press Freedom

- ARTICLE 19
- The Committee to Protect Journalists
- Electronic Frontier Foundation
- International Freedom of Expression Exchange
- Internationale Medienhilfe
- International Press Institute
- OSCE Representative on Freedom of the Media
- Reporters Without Borders
- World Association of Newspapers
- World Press Freedom Committee
- Worldwide Governance Indicators
- Student Press Law Center

REFERENCES

Bagdikian, Ben H. (2004). *The new media monopoly*. Boston: Beacon Press.

Barker, Michael (2007). "Conform or Reform? Social Movements and the Mass Media", *Fifth-Estate-Online - International Journal of Radical Mass Media Criticism.*

Barker, Michael (2008). "The Liberal Foundations of Media Reform? Creating Sustainable Funding Opportunities for Radical Media Reform", *Global Media Journal*, 1 (2), June 2008.

Brennan Center for Justice, NYU School of Law, The Free expression Policy Project. (2006). *Fact sheets on media democracy.*

Bruns, Axel (2006). "Wikinews: The Next Generation of Alternative Online News?" *Scan Journal* 3(1)

Chester, Jeffrey, & Larson, Gary O. (July 23, 2002). A 12-step programme for media democracy. The Nation Online.

Dichter, Aliza. (2003). Is this what media democracy looks like?. Media Development. 2003/4.

Gillmor, Dan. (2004). *We the media: Grassroots journalism by the people, for the people.* O'Reilly Media.

Hackett, Robert A. & Carroll, William K. (2004) Critical social movements and media reform. *Media Development.* 2004/1.

Hackett, Robert A. & Carroll, William K. (2006). *Remaking Media: The Sturggle to Democratize Public Communication.* New York; London: Routledge

Hackett, Robert A. (2000) "Taking Back the Media: Notes on the Potential for a Communicative Democracy Movement," *Studies in Political Economy: A Socialist Review* 63(3) pp. 61-86.

Hackett, Robert A. (2001). Building a Movement for Media Democratisation. In P. Phillips and Project Censored. *Project Censored 2001*. New York : Seven Stories.

Hazen, Don and Julie Winokur, (eds). (1997) *We the Media: A Citizens' Guide to Fighting for Media Democracy.* New York: The New Press.

Lewis, Jeff (2005) *Language Wars: The Role of Media and Culture in Global Terror and Political Violence,* London: University of Michigan Press/ Pluto Books.

McChesney, Robert W. and Nichols, John (2002) Our Media, Not theirs: The Democratic Struggle Against Corporate Media. New York : Seven Stories.

Schiff, Stacy (July 31, 2006). "Know It All: Can Wikipedia Conquer Expertise?" *The New Yorker*.

Shariatmadari, David (2006). "Is a Million Articles Proof of Authentic Information?" Intermedia (Vol. 34, Iss. 3): p. 17-18.

Glossary

Alpha test: In software development, an early stage of testing by in-house personnel to identify bugs in the program. It usually involves systematically trying out all of a program's functions.

Animated GIF: A GIF graphic file, which consists of two or more images shown in a timed sequence to give the effect of motion.

anonymous ftp: A traditional form of login to a public ftp site where the username is given as 'anonymous' and the password is your e-mail address, for example 'walthowe@delphiforums.com'.

API: Application Program Interface. An interface between the operating system and application programs that specifies how the two communicate with each other.

applet: An application that is downloaded from a web page and executed by browser software. Also, an HTML tag that defines an applet program.

archie: One of the first search engines introduced to the nets, developed by Peter Deutsch and others at McGill U. Archie is software that indexes thousands of ftp sites and lets you search for the files and software that you want. It was short for "archiver", protested Deutsch, after the search tools VERONICA and JUGhead followed it.

archive: 1. A storage repository for software, data, or other materials to be saved and preserved. 2. A technique of combining multiple files into a single file to enable easier backup, handling or transmission. Some of the software programs used to archive files are PKZIP, WinZip, Stuffit, and tar. Files with the following extensions are likely to be archived: sea, tar, taz, taZ, tgz, and zip. See compression.

ARPANET : The network created by the Advanced Research Projects Agency (ARPA) that became the Internet. See the Internet History

ASCII art: Artwork composed entirely of ASCII characters used as lines and shapes, not as characters with meanings. The simplest ASCII art is the simple smiley faces, but at the other end of the scale, they can be large, elaborate pictures. For a good collection of ASCII art, see the ASCII Dictionary

ASCII file: ASCII files are those that only use the 128 characters that can be encoded with 7 binary digits. This means that most text files are ASCII files. Word processed files, which include special characters and control codes are usually encoded with 8 binary digits. Some Internet protocols only support 7-bit text, such as simple mailers and newsgroups. Because of this, ways have been developed to encode binary files into ASCII form. The most common of these are uuencode and binhex, the latter for Macintosh files, primarily. Two more examples of 7-bit file systems are postscript(.ps files) and TeX (.tex files), which are word processing systems that allow encoding of complex information in 7-bit form. Common extensions for ASCII files are .txt, .uue, .xxe, .hqx, .ps, and .tex. Also files with names like README or index are almost always text files. The .doc extension may be text or may be 8-bit, and you need to know more about it to be sure.

ASCII: American Standard Code for Information Interchange. A standard way to encode upper and lower case letters in the English alphabet, numbers, and special characters using only seven bits, and therefore limited to 128 characters. The basis for coding simple text files. See ASCII Table. To provide more characters, such as accented characters and mathematical symbols, an 8th bit is often added, providing 256 characters in all. There are different standard 256 character sets, but the most common is ISO Latin 1 (ISO 8859-1) used on the web.

ATM: Asynchronous Transfer Mode. A packet switching model for fast long distance communications that uses fixed packet size and allows for intelligent decisions on routing, handling, prioritization, and costing. This allows for special handling and routing for data that must be reassembled quickly and accurately, such as live Video. See differentiated service.

B2B: Business to Business. A mode of conducting business between two or more companies over the Internet, rather than more traditional modes such as telephone, mail, and face to face.

B2R: Back to Reality!

Backbon: A central network connecting other networks together. Formerly a network run by the National Science Foundation for the US, there are now multiple backbones run by commercial providers such as MCI, Sprint, UUNET, and AT&T.

bandwidth: Literally, the frequency width of a transmission channel in Hertz, kiloHertz, megaHertz, etc. Often used as an expression of the amount of data that can be sent through a circuit. The greater the bandwidth, the greater the amount of data that can travel in a given time period. See broadband.

Bang address: An old system of mail addressing in UUCP networks, where the successive routing addresses were followed by exclamation points (also known as bangs) and the addressee was the last element.

Baud rate B2B: A nearly obsolete term for transmission rates synonymous in early, simple systems with bits per second. In faster, more complex systems of encoding and transmitting data, the term loses its simple meaning and has fallen into disuse (and frequent misuse). See baud.

Baud: Rate of transmission speed in a signal - the number of changes of state, such as voltage or frequency, per second in a signal. Named for the French teleprinter inventor Baudot. In simplest systems, it is synonymous with bits per second. In more complex systems, a baud may include more than one bit.

Baudot code: The Baudot code, used by early teleprinters, represents letters, numbers, and symbols in five-character binary codes, which includes shifts to increase the number of characters beyond 32.

BBS: Bulletin Board System. A dial-up service offering messages, files, and other services over a modem. BBS were very popular in the 1980s and early 1990s, but have been largely replaced by the Internet.

Bcc: Blind Carbon Copy. Unlike the Cc option (Carbon Copy), when the Bcc address option is selected in e-mail, other addressees do not see the Bcc address.

beta test: In software development, a stage of testing where the program is tried out with a selected trial audience to find and correct bugs, usually people of similar backgrounds to those expected to use the software. Check out Delphi's Beta Test Forum. Compare to alpha test.

Binary: Binary means the use of only two values, zero and one, in encoding data. All digital computers primarily use some form of binary encoding, such as 8 or 16 or 32 binary digits at a time. Characters that you see on screen or type with your keyboard are normally encoded with 8 binary digits. For example, the binary value for the letter A is 01000001.

Binary files: Binary files are files that include up to 256 different characters and are encoded by 8 binary digits (bits) for each character. Simple text or ASCII files only use 128 different characters and can be encoded by 7 binary digits. Examples of binary files are most programs, most word- processed files, most graphics files, and most sound files. If you don't know a file is ASCII, it is probably a binary file.

Bit: Short for binary digit (0 or 1). Lower case b is used in abbreviations to distinguish it from bytes. For example, KBps (thousand bytes per second) is 8 times as great as Kbps (thousand bits per second).

Bitmap: A graphic which is defined by specifying the colors of dots or pixels which make up the picture. Also known as raster graphics. Common types of bitmap graphics are GIF, JPEG, Photoshop, PCX, TIFF, Macintosh Paint, Microsoft Paint, BMP, PNG, FAX formats, and TGA. See vector graphics for a different type of graphic and metafiles for a combination of the two types.

Blog: Short for web log; usually a chronological record of thoughts, links, events, or actions posted on the web. For examples, see the Yahoo Directory of Weblogs. For another point of view, see John Dvorak's Deconstructing a Blog.

BOFH: "Bastard Operator From Hell," a classic diary of the ultimate in outrageous system support widely posted on Usenet. Always worth a return visit.

Bookmark: Just as a paper bookmark is used as a reminder of the page you are on in a book, electronic bookmarks are used to bring you back to a website or other site you may want to return to. The Netscape browser lets you bookmark any site and save the bookmarks in a file you can recall at any time. Microsoft Internet Explorer uses the term "favorite" instead of bookmark for the same concept.

Boolean search: A method of searching for information in databases that combines search terms with the operators AND, OR, NOT, and parentheses. See a fuller explanation in our file, What is Boolean Searching?

Bot: Short for robot, a program designed to search the Internet looking for information. A common use of bots is the variously named spiders, worms, and crawlers that support search engines by following links from site to site and within a site to dig out information to be indexed by the search engine. Another is the MusicBot™ used by BMI to find who is putting unlicensed, copyrighted music on web pages.

Bounce: The return of an e-mail message because of an error in its address or delivery.

Bridge: A bridge is a combination of hardware and software that connects local area networks (LANs) of similar types together. See router.

Broadband: When the bandwidth of a signal is large, it can simultaneously carry many channels of information. Fiber optic cable, in particular, has a very high bandwidth, and is referred to as broadband.

Browser: Software that will load and display a web page. A browser interprets the HTML or XML code from the web page files, executes embedded scripts and programs, provides encryption/decryption for security where needed, displays graphics (except text-only browsers), plays music and video, and provides links to related pages. Browsers are purportedly based on standards developed by the World Wide Web Consortium and recognized by the Internet Engineering Task Force. The major browser software developers participate in these organizations, but each of them also builds in their own proprietary codes, whether or not approved by the organizations. These differences in browsers create a challenge for web page developers. The principle browsers are Netscape, Microsoft Internet Explorer, Opera, Mosaic, and the text-only Lynx. See the Internet Software Guide.

Bus : An electronic pathway. In networks, a configuration (topology) with a single linear cable, terminated at each end, to which computers and devices are connected. There are no loops or branches in the cable. Also called a daisy chain.

Byte: 8 bits of data. Capital B is used in abbreviations to distinguish it from bits. For example, KBps (thousand bytes per second) is 8 times as great as Kbps (thousand bits per second).

Certificate authority: An organisation that issues digital certificates. A CA is responsible for guaranteeing a certificate holder's identity.

CGI(Common Gateway Interface): A specification for transferring information between a Webserver and a CGI program. The programs cam be written in any language like C, Perl, Visual Basic, Java, as long as it conforms to CGI specifications. CGI makes it possible for Webservers to dynamically interact with users. The most common use of CGI is seen in online forms.

Client: When you access a service on a computer, then your computer is the client, while the other one is called the server. Services include file and print, e-mail, Web, etc.

DHCP (Dynamic Host Configuration Protocol): A protocol used for dynamically assigning IP addresses to clients that request for it. When configuring a DHCP server, a pool or range of IP addresses has to be given. The server then uses DHCP to assign the IP addresses from this pool.

DHTML (Dynamic HTML): Refers to Web pages, that change their contents depending on client requests.

Digital certificate: An attachment sent along with a message for authentication purposes. A digital certificate verifies that the user sending the message is *who* he or she claims to be.

Directory service: A service that stores information on the network in a hierarchical format for easy accessibility. It can store information about applications, equipment, and users on a network.

DNS (Domain Name System): A system used on the Internet to translate IP addresses into easy to remember names. The service that does this translation is called DNS. DNS servers are connected with each other over the Internet. So, if one DNS server doesn't have an IP address translation in its table, it queries other systems running DNS to find out.

Domain; A group of computers that function under common, rules. On the Internet, it's put as an extension in a host name for identifying the type of host. Various domain types have been identified. These include .com (company/commercial), .edu (educational institutions), .gov (government), .mil (military), .org (organisation). Outside the US, she domain name is a 2-letter country code (.in for India).

Download: To copy a file from a remote machine, for example, with anonymous FTP, or when you want to copy a program from a Website and save it to your hard disk.

Finger: A standard utility that is part of the TCP/IP protocol stack that lets you determine who is a valid user and who is logged into a system you have access to. It's used in UNIX based systems. The syntax is finger username@domain. name, or fingei@host:

Firewall: A system to prevent unauthorised access to a private network. A firewall is used on a network directly connected to the Internet to prevent outside internet users from accessing it.

Freeware: Software that is distributed free of charge, but often without customer service or much documentation.

FTP (File Transfer Protocol): A simple program to transfer files over a network from one computer to another. Many FT? servers allow you to download files without having an account on the machine, by using anonymous or FTP for a user name and your e-mail address as a password. This is a major means of distributing software and info on the Internet.

Gateway: A device that is connected to the Internet, and allows other machines inside a company's network to access the Internet. In other words, it's the connection point between a LAN and the internet. The device can be a specialised piece of hardware like a router, or it can be software installed on a computer.

GIF (Graphics Interchange Format): A standard graphics image format used on the Internet.

Gopher: A menu-based system for organising and distributing information on the Internet. It's similar to FTP as it lets users browse or download files and directories. A key feature of Gopher is the ability to include menu items that connect the user to other Gopher servers. Gopher is no longer in popular use.

Guest: When you connect to or log onto a remote computer on which you don't have your own account, (perhaps using a special account for guests) you are referred to as a guest or visitor.

Hacker: Originally, this term referred to crackerjack programmers and computer experts and connoted respect. Though this meaning is still in use, this word is now also used (especially by the media) to refer to people who deliberately try to penetrate the security of other computers. The computer user community prefers to call these people crackers.

Header: Information in the beginning of a piece of data being sent over a network that describes its content, the destination address, etc.

Homepage: An HTML document that serves as the main access point to a company's Website.

HTML (Hypertext Markup Language): A simple and easy to learn programming language that Web documents are written in.

HTTP (HyperText Transfer Protocol): The protocol used on the Internet to transfer HTML documents. All Web browsers use this protocol to read the Web pages.

Hypertext: A new concept for organising information made possible by computers, where keywords or phrases can be used not only to reference additional resources, but also serve as software links to these resources.

IMAP4: The Internet Message Access Protocol lets you view your e-mail at the server treating the server mailbox as an extension of your computer. You can view, delete and search for mail on the server, and only download the ones you need to your local machine.

Interface: The manner in which a user provides information to a computer program. Some examples are GUI for graphical user interface, and CLI for command line interface.

Internet: The Internet is the Grand Daddy of all networks. It's a collection of computers and computer networks across the world that communicate across dedicated high-speed phone lines using a single protocol family called TCP/ IP.

IP address: A unique set of four numbers between 1 and 254 separated by periods, such as 209.194.84.60, used to identify every machine connected to the Internet. As these numbers are very difficult to remember, they are mapped to an easy to remember name, which is called the host name.

IRC (Internet Relay Chat): A program that allows multiple users to conduct typed conversations in real time over the Internet.

ISO (International Organisation for Standardisation): An international body made up of national standard bodies from over 75 countries. It's engaged indefining Standards. The most popular computer standard defined by ISO was the OSI model.

ITU (International Telecommunications Union): An international body engaged in defining telecommunication standards.

JPEG (Joint Photographies Expert Group): A standard (compressed) format for color images commonly used on the Internet. They use the JPC or JPEG extensions.

Jughead (Jonzy's universal gopher hierarchy excavation and display): A pow-erful gopher search tool written by Rhett "Jonzy" Jones.

Kermit: A simple modem protocol for transferring files between Macs and/or PCs, or from these to bigger computers. Since TCP/IP was adopted as the official Internet protocol in 1983, most PC software has abandoned Kermit. However, Kermit and its cousins X-, Y-, and Z-modem are still needed in the absence of an ethernet or SLIP connection.

LDAP (Lightweight Directory Access Protocol): A set of protocols for querying information directories. There are various directory services on the Internet that can be queried for information. LDAP is being used in operating systems like the upcoming Windows 2000 and NetWare for querying their directory services. LDAP is a simpler version of the X.500 directory service standard.

Lynx: A text only Web browser.

Mailing list: A mechanism for simultaneously distributing e-mail messages to a group of e-mail users who have subscribed to the list. A common use of mailing lists is in newsletter subscriptions.

MIME (Multipurpose Internet Mail Extensions): A way to encapsulate binary file attachments, such as images and sounds into e-mail messages. The method was originally suggested in RFC-1341.

Mirror site: A site that is the exact replica of another site. This is used by various anonymous FTP sites to reduce bandwidth bottlenecks, so that more users can access it.

MP3(MPEG1 Layer 3): A new format for storing audio information that is becoming very popular on the Internet. It achieves very high compression ratios, and gives high quality playback. Some shareware MP3 players are available on the Internet. There is an upgrade to the Windows Media Player that also supports this standard.

Multilink PPP: A protocol that combines the bandwidths of multiple PPP links to give greater throughputs.

Netiquette: The etiquette of communicating over the Internet. The Internet community follows various conventions when transmitting information over the Internet. For example, sending a message in all caps is the equivalent of shouting.

Newsgroup: A UseNet discussion group or bulletin board. Users can subscribe to newsgroups, and then see all or post messages on it.

NSFNET: The backbone of the Internet since 1990 when ARPANET was dismantled. It originally linked six supercomputers through high-speed phone lines.

Online: A standard terminology that indicates whether an Internet connection is live or not.

PINE (Pine Is Not Elm): A sophisticated e-mail utility that can send not only text files, but also binary files, such as images and sounds by using MIME.

Ping (Packet Internet Gopher): A utility that checks whether a host on the Internet is accessible or not. It's mostly used to troubleshoot connectivity issues on the Internet.

PNG (Portable Network Graphics): A new graphics format that is becoming popular on the Internet.

Port: A 16-bit number used by a server to identify itself to clients. A client connecting to a computer uses an IP address as well as a port number to talk to a particular server.

PPP (Point-to-Point Protocol): A protocol that dynamically assigns an IP address to a computer, so that it can access the Internet.

Public Key Infrastructure (PKI): A technique that uses digital certificates to verify the authenticity of all parties involved in an Internet transaction.

Public/private key encryption: A cryptographic algorithm which uses two keys, one to encrypt and the other to decrypt the data.

Pull technology: The opposite of Push technology in which information is only provided when a client requests for it. The Web functions on pull technology where a browser sends a request to a Website for information. ;

Push technology: A technology being used on the Internet in which a server sends out information to the client without the client requesting for it. The most common use of the technology is seen in subscribing to newsletters, where news is sent to the registered clients without requesting for it.

RFCs (Request For Comments): The working notes of the committees that develop the protocols and standards of the Internet, including proposed changes. These documents contain a great deal of info about the Net and are maintained by the Internet Activities Board (IAB).

Server: A computer in a network that provides access to other computers in the network to programs, web pages, data, or other files and services, such as printer access or communications access. A server may also authenticate requests for files and services before providing them. See also proxy server and client-server architecture.

SGML: Acronym for Standard Graphics Markup Language. It was adopted in 1986 as an international standard (ISO 8879) for the creation, management, storage, and delivery of information products. HTML and its possible successor, XML, are both subsets of SGML. See the SGML/XML Home Page for more information.

Shareware: Software that is offered for free download in hopes that the user will decide to keep it and pay a fee for it after trying it out. See freeware.

Shell, shell account: An Internet account, usually unix based, that provides the Internet software for you. In contrast, SLIP, PPP, and ethernet accounts give you a connection where you run your own Internet software, such as browsers, gopher, telnet, e-mail, and so on. Shell accounts run these for you, and usually only provide text modes without graphics. Most shell accounts require some knowledge of unix commands, although many functions can be set up in friendly menu structures. A shell account can be based in VMS, as well, such as Delphi Internet Service's older textside access.

Site: A host on the Internet which allows remote access by such protocols as http, ftp, telnet, or gopher. A site may consist of a single page or many pages under a common site name. Whether two addresses with a common site name are one site or more than one may vary depending on your point of view. For example, to some, all pages at the Internet Service Provider delphiforums.com might be considered one site. But an individual who has set up personal web pages at people.delphiforums.com will refer to his or her pages as "my web site."

Slam, slamming: Slamming is the practice of telephone companies shifting you to their long distance service without your permission or obtaining your permission deceptively.

SLIP: Serial Line Interface Protocol. Along with the newer PPP, a protocol that can be used with a dialup connection to an ISP to complete a TCP/IP Internet connection.

SMTP: Simple Mail Transfer Protocol. The protocol used to send mail between servers and to send mail from your client to a mail server. Your address to send mail using software like Eudora, Pegasus, or the mail clients in Netscape and MSIE will often begin with smtp. For Delphi, the address to send mail through is smtp.delphiforums.com. See POP.

Social engineering: A cracker term for tricking users of a system to reveal passwords so that the cracker can gain entry to the system. A common technique is to contact users in chat or e-mail on a system, pretend that they are employees of the system performing security checks, and insist that the users give their password to prove who they are or their account will be closed. Such requests are never legitimate! Social engineering schemes can be quite ingenious and convincing and more subtle than the simple technique above. Never reveal a password or even give hints what it may be.

Spam: Traditionally, spam is flooding message boards, newsgroups, mailing lists, or your mailbox with unwanted, unsolicited off-topic messages—usually ads or promotions or deliberate disruptions. It is a major violation of netiquette, and it violates member agreements in most places and can lead to account cancellation. While spam is usually viewed as large numbers of messages, to the individual, one unwanted message is spam. The term was inspired by an old Monty Python sketch about a repetitive menu with spam, spam, eggs, and spam.

Spider: A software robot that serves a search engine by

exploring the net, collecting web page addresses and page contents, and following links from them to other addresses to collect still more web information. Also known as a worm or crawler. See search engine.

Spim: Spam sent by instant messaging.

Spyware: Software planted on your system to capture and reveal information to someone outside your system. It can do such things as capture your keystrokes while typing passwords, read and track your e-mail, record what sites you visit, pass along credit card numbers and so on. It can be planted by Trojan horses or viruses, installed as part of freeware or shareware programs you download and run, installed by an employer to track your computer usage, or even planted by advertising agencies to assist in feeding you targeted ads.

SSL: Secure Sockets Layer. A security protocol developed by Netscape for commercial transactions on the Internet. Using public-key cryptography, it provides server authentication, data encryption, and data integrity. You can recognize its use with URLs beginning https instead of http.

Star: A network configuration (topology) in which all computers and devices are connected by direct cables to a central hub.

Stopword: Stopwords are very commonly used words that are normally excluded from automated searches. Examples: a, an, the, for, to, in, on, and, etc.

Streaming audio, streaming video: Technologies which permit listening and watching continuously as the signal is transferred to your system from a remote web site. It requires a high degree of compression to transfer audio or video (or both) at 28.8 Kbps or

14.4 Kbps speeds and still retain quality music and non-jerky video. If stereo sound is desired, there is a trade-off in the sound quality. These technologies are continually improving and the sound and video sampling and compression techniques are getting better. Faster connection speeds are needed to improve quality substantially, and the speed must be maintained over the entire path between the transmitting and receiving systems. The systems generally use a few seconds buffering, but signal slowdowns or interruptions longer than that break the flow.

Surf: To explore the nets without any more specific a purpose than to see what is out there.

SVG: Scalable Vector Graphics. A proposed format by the World Wide Web Consortium (W3C) for web page graphics based on vectors, rather than bitmap formats. These files will normally be smaller than bitmap files and will scale to different size screens. See the W3C Scalable Vector Graphics page.

TCP/IP (Transmission Control Protocol/ Internet Protocol): A family of protocols used over the Internet. This family includes protocols for handling data transport (TCP, UDP), routing (IP, ICMP, RIP, OSPF), addresses (ARP, DNS, RARP), user services (BOOTP, FTP, TELNET), gateways (EGP, GGP, IGP), and other services (NFS, NIS, RFC, SMTP, SNMP).

Telnet: A utility to log onto a remote computer.

Tunneling: A method used to connect two points using the Internet as the channel. VPNs use tunneling to establish connections between different computers. The tunneling is done using various tunneling protocols like PPTP, L2F, IPSec, etc. These protocols encapsulate the data inside the TCP/IP protocol so that it can be sent over the Internet. Some of these protocols like IP Sec also encrypt the data before sending it for security.

URL (Universal Resource Locator): The mechanism used by the Internet to find a particular page, image, or sound. Simply speaking, it's an address for the page.

UseNet (Users' Network): A text-based mechanism that supports discussion groups known as newsgroups, that allow users from anywhere on the Internet to participate. Contrary to the name, it's not actually a network but a service available on the Internet.

uuencode (Unix-to-Unix encoding): A UNIX utility for converting binary files to ASCII for transmission via e-mail between UNIX machines. On the receiving end, uudecode is used to convert back to binary.

Veronica (Very Easy Rodent-Oriented Net-wide Index to Computerised Archives): A search tool for use with Gophers (a rodent).

VPN (Virtual Private Networking): A technology that allows interconnectivity between networks or between mobile users and a network using the Internet backbone as the media for transferring the data.

W3C: The World Wide Web Consortium is an international organisation involved in creating and maintaining most Web-based standards.

WAIS (Wide Area Information Servers): Using keywords supplied by the user, WAIS servers search their databases for any files which contain a match. WAIS goes Beyond Gopher, FTP, and Archie searches, but is somewhat similar to WebCrawler.

Web browser: An application for browsing the Internet. These browsers can read both HTTP and FTP Websites. There are many popular Web browsers around like Netscape Communicator, and Internet Explorer.

Web page: A page written in Hyper-Text Markup Language that's available on the Internet through the HTTP protocol.

Website: A site consisting of various Web pages that can be accessed by anyone connected to the Internet.

WWW (World Wide Web): Now more commonly known as the Web. It's a system that lets users graphically browse through sites on the Internet, and follow pointers (called links or hyperlinks) to other documents that can be anywhere.

X.500: An ISO and ITU standard that defines how a directory service should be structured.

XML (Extensible Markup Language): A new scripting language being developed by the W3C (World Wide Web Consortium) which provides more functionality than HTML.

Z39.50: "American National Standard Z39.50: Information Retrieval Service Definition and Protocol Specification for Library Applications." This was designed to be a standard for connecting library computers and databases regardless of hardware and software. It could be used as a standard for many kinds of databases. It has not caught on, and there are many, many other database protocols in use today in and out of libraries.

Zip: A method of file compression originally used with MSDOS and a file extension for files which are zip compressed.

Zmodem: A very common form of file transmission, which can be used across dialup and telnet connections. It can be used in batch modes (for multiple files), and it is faster than the older xmodem and ymodem. In some implementations, it can resume a transfer after a connection has been broken and re-established.

Bibliography

Bagdikian, Ben H. (2004). *The New Media Monopoly.* Boston: Beacon Press.

Barker, Michael (2007). "Conform or Reform? Social Movements and the Mass Media", *Fifth-Estate-Online International Journal of Radical Mass Media Criticism.*

Barker, Michael (2008). "The Liberal Foundations of Media Reform? Creating Sustainable Funding Opportunities for Radical Media Reform", *Global Media Journal,* 1 (2), June 2008.

Bhatia, Arun (2005). *Computer Mediated Communication,* Akansha, New Delhi.

Brennan Center for Justice, NYU School of Law, The Free expression Policy Project. (2006). *Fact sheets on media democracy.*

Bruns, Axel (2006). "Wikinews: The Next Generation of Alternative Online News?" *Scan Journal* 3(1)

Chambers and Tinckell (1998) Angocentric versions of the international: the privileging of Anglo-ethnicity in cultural studies and the global media. 21st conference of IAMCR, Glasgow.

Chester, Jeffrey, & Larson, Gary O. (July 23, 2002). A 12-step programme for media democracy. *The Nation Online.*

Datta, K.B. (2008). *History of Journalism,* Akansha, New Delhi.

Dichter, Aliza. (2003). Is this what media democracy looks like?. *Media Development.* 2003/4.

Eskilson, Stephen J. (2007). *Graphic Design: A New History*. New Haven, Connecticut: Yale University Press.

Gillmor, Dan. (2004). *We the media: Grassroots journalism by the people, for the people*. O'Reilly Media.

Gupta, D.K. (2005). *Modern Encyclopaedia of Meida and Mass Communicaiton,* Rajat, New Delhi.

Hackett, Robert A. & Carroll, William K. (2004) Critical social movements and media reform. *Media Development.* 2004/1.

Hackett, Robert A. & Carroll, William K. (2006). *Remaking Media: The Sturggle to Democratize Public Communication*. New York; London: Routledge

Hackett, Robert A. (2000) "Taking Back the Media: Notes on the Potential for a Communicative Democracy Movement," *Studies in Political Economy: A Socialist Review* 63(3) pp. 61-86.

Hackett, Robert A. (2001). Building a Movement for Media Democratisation. In P. Phillips and Project Censored. Project Censored 2001. New York : Seven Stories.

Hazen, Don and Julie Winokur, (eds). (1997) *We the Media: A Citizens' Guide to Fighting for Media Democracy.* New York: The New Press.

Lewis, Jeff (2005) *Language Wars: The Role of Media and Culture in Global Terror and Political Violence,* London: University of Michigan Press/ Pluto Books.

Liberman, Mark (2005-12-23). "Multiplying ideologies considered harmful". Language Log. http://itre.cis.upenn.edu/~myl/languagelog/archives/002724.html.

McChesney, Robert W. and Nichols, John (2002) *Our Media, Not theirs: The Democratic Struggle Against Corporate Media.* New York : Seven Stories.

McChesney, Robert Waterman. (2000). *Rich media, poor democracy: Communication politics in dubious times.* New York: New Press.

McChesney, Robert, *Educators and the Battle for Control of U.S. Broadcasting, 1928-35*, Rich Media, Poor Democracy,

Robins, Susan P., *Encyclopedia of Social Work,* 19th Edition, National Association of Social Workers. Washington, DC. 1997 Update.

Ronald Bailey, *Global Warming and Other Eco Myths: How the Environmental Movement Uses False Science to Scare Us to Death*, Prima Lifestyles; 2002.

Schiff, Stacy (July 31, 2006). "Know It All: Can Wikipedia Conquer Expertise?" *The New Yorker.*

Shariatmadari, David (2006). "Is a Million Articles Proof of Authentic Information?" *Intermedia* (Vol. 34, Iss. 3): p. 17-18.

Taylor, Alan. (2005). We, the media:Pedagogic Intrusions into US FIlm and Broadcast News Rhetorics. Peter Lang Frankfurt / New York. http://wethemedia.edublogs.org

Weatherly, Jeffrey N, et al. (2007), "Perceptions of Political Bias in the Headlines of Two Major News Organizations," *The Harvard International Journal of Press/Politics*(12), 91, p. 97.

Index

bytes per second) is 8 times as great as Kbps (thousand bits per second).

Certificate authority: An organization that issues digital certificates. A CA is responsible for guaranteeing a certificate holder's identity.

CGI(Common Gateway Interface): A specification for transferring information between a Webserver and a CGI program. The programs can be written in any language like C, Perl, Visual Basic, Java, as long as it conforms to CGI specifications. CGI makes it possible for Webservers to dynamically interact with users. The most common use of CGI is seen in online forms.

Client: When you access a service on a computer, then your computer is the client, while the other one is called the server. Services include file and print, mail, Web, etc.

DHCP (Dynamic Host Configuration Protocol): A protocol used for dynamically assigning IP addresses to clients that request for it. When configuring a DHCP server, a pool or range of IP addresses has to be given. The server then uses DHCP to assign the IP addresses from this pool.

DHTML (Dynamic HTML): Refers to Web pages, that change their contents depending on client requests.

Digital certificate: An attachment sent along with a message for authentication purposes. A digital certificate verifies that the user sending the message is *who* he or she claims to be.

Directory service: A service that stores information on the network in a hierarchical format for easy accessibility. It can store information about applications, equipment, and users on a network.